"Beginners preach from the obscure texts; veterans from the more familiar ones. Louis Simon combines the best of both by making the home shores strange and obscuring the familiar so that it can become fresh again. This book of virtuoso sermons may well be the best cure for claustrophobic Christianity out there. Pick up *"My" Jesus* and start anywhere and find out why two distinguished philosophers, Paul Ricoeur and Charles Courtney, would invest their talents in making these masterpieces available to a wider audience."

—LEONARD SWEET
Professor, Drew University and George Fox University

"This remarkable collection of newly translated sermons comes from another time and place-Protestant France of two generations ago. Reading good sermons from outside one's context tends to jostle all the current assumptions how familiar Bible texts should be understood and preached. In sermon after sermon, Louis Simon takes the familiar, turns it on its head, and leaves the reader nodding and whispering, 'Just so, just so.'"

—MICHAEL L. LINDVALL
Senior Minister of the Brick Presbyterian Church, New York City

"My" Jesus

"My" Jesus

Meditations on Gospel Texts

By
LOUIS SIMON

FOREWORD by Paul Ricoeur
TRANSLATED by Charles Courtney

WIPF & STOCK · Eugene, Oregon

"MY" JESUS
Meditations on Gospel Texts

Translation copyright © 2011 Charles Courtney. Original French edition copyright Editions Olivetan, Lyon France www.editions-olivetan.com. All rights reserved. Except for brief quotations in critical publications or reviews, no part of this book may be reproduced in any manner without prior written permission from the publisher. Write: Permissions, Wipf and Stock Publishers, 199 W. 8th Ave., Suite 3, Eugene, OR 97401.

Cover photo of the 11th Century Romanesque church in Saint-Martin-de-Londres, France, by Francis de Richemond.

Wipf & Stock
An Imprint of Wipf and Stock Publishers
199 W. 8th Ave., Suite 3
Eugene, OR 97401

www.wipfandstock.com

ISBN 13: 978-1-61097-397-7

Manufactured in the U.S.A.

Contents

Foreword by Paul Ricoeur / vii
Preface / xiii

1. Two Unfinished Parables: The Treasure and the Pearl (Matthew 13:44–46) / 1
2. The Companions of Jesus (Luke 14:16–24) / 6
3. Did Jesus Speak with Authority? (Mark 1:21–28) / 10
4. Pamphlet Against the Pious (Luke 10:29–37) / 16
5. Zacchaeus Climbs a Tree (Luke 19:1–10) / 22
6. The Temptation to Do Good (Mark 1:40–45) / 27
7. Is Leprosy Contagious? (Matthew 8:1–4) / 33
8. Jesus the Provocateur (Mark 2:13–18a) / 39
9. A Festival of Birds (Mark 4:30–32) / 44
10. Jerusalem Prayers Go Round and Round (Luke 18:9–14) / 48
11. The True Vine (John 14:31—15:8) / 53
12. The Gospel Begins at Cana (John 2:1–11) / 58
13. Zechariah, the Mute Prophet (Luke 1:5–23) / 64
14. A Healing of Communication (Luke 7:1–10) / 70
15. The Widow's Last Penny (Mark 12:41–44) / 78

16 The Shepherd (John 10:1–6, 22) / 84

17 Sower, Nothing but the Sower (Mark 4:3–9) / 91

18 No More Cursed Fig Trees! (Luke 13:6–9) / 97

19 A Story of Adultery (John 8:3–11) / 103

20 My Lord: It Is Like a Man Going on a Journey . . . (Mark 13:33–37) / 109

21 Christ Is Born in Pagan Territory (Mark 7:24—9:10) / 115

22 The Temple Veil Torn from Top to Bottom (Mark 15:33–38) / 122

23 Easter: His Body Has Disappeared! (Mark 16:1–8) / 129

Foreword

WHEN THE parable speaks again.

I will not hide my emotional response to reading these lively and incisive texts of Louis Simon. When he speaks of "his" Jesus—in order to share him with others, I hear "my" pastor of the years at Palaiseau. It was a time when protestant preaching was seeking the right tone between railing against the powers that be and prudently taking shelter behind the walls of tradition. Today, when I read the sermons gathered here, I hear them and I listen to them once again.

In these introductory pages, my main purpose is to gather for the readers some of the fruits of my harvest. But I will also attempt to project these texts out ahead of themselves and for other times.

What is proposed here is a "stripped down" reading of the Gospel, parallel to what was sought in Romanesque art, evoked by the photograph on the book's cover. The proximity of Jesus, signified by the audacious and yet modest "my" of the title, is not an affected tenderness: it is inseparable from the grandeur of the Gospel of this Jesus. This grandeur is signified by the extravagance of the parables, of the new commandments, and the scandalous behavior and unusual encounters reported by the Gospels. So, proximity of the person, but extremism of the preaching spoken and acted out—that is the paradoxical equation around which this collection turns. What balances the equation, one can say, is the authority of the words and acts of Jesus. Louis Simon sees this authority constantly engaged in a no-holds-barred polemic with "the religious types": experts in doctrine, those stingy with compassion, enamored with ritual, and refugees in the imaginary of invisible worlds. Zacchaeus, rich and religious, must come down from his tree and receive Jesus in his house; having done so, Zacchaeus "abandoned religion for the Gospel." The shepherd of evangelical proclamation is not the herdsman put in charge of the frightened lambs, but the one who pushes the sheep out of the fold. The gospel shepherd is a master figure of rupture. As for the disciples, they understand . . . nothing. The redaction process of the gospels sometimes reveals the domestication of the novelty of the Gospel: the Parable of the Sower becomes the allegory of the different soils; Jesus speaks as a poet and people hear only a scholar. If the parable upsets, the allegory reassures. Because of this, the task of preaching is to bring the parable to speech and to bring out its sharpness. Thus the sower is seen to be one who simply sows without concern for the harvest. One is ready to side with the worker who disobeys the master who has told him to dig up the sterile fig tree; the worker pleads for the trees, for patience. And what are we to do with all the parables in which the master goes on a trip? How can we maintain rapport with a Lord who gives up closeness with others, the little ones and the poor? Louis Simon risks saying, "God has created humans like the ocean creates its continents, by withdrawing." We are not abandoned, but free and adults. I also love the commentary on the Parable of the Mustard Seed which puts forth "large branches" for a festival of birds, but not a tree "huge and glorious like a cedar." What a shortcut from the seed to the birds!

But the greatest reward from my reading has been to be able to bring together in a single sheaf three woman figures, which I will evoke one by one. First is the adulterous woman who put to flight the accusers ready to stone her: "In each self-righteous person who thinks that they are impeccable sleeps a murderer," thunders Louis Simon. Next is the Syro-Phoenician woman, encountered in a pagan country, who teaches Jesus a lesson: even the dogs under the table eat the children's crumbs. This woman converts a Jesus still too Jewish to be an audacious crosser of boundaries toward the stranger. Louis Simon dares to say that this opening of Jesus to pagans "gives birth to the universal Christ, the Christ for others." There is no other Christ in this collection of sermons. I am pleased finally to point to the figure of the widow who gives out of her poverty, puts in everything she had, her whole living. And Louis Simon declares: "Jesus died like the widow."

This astonishing affirmation leads to the heart of Louis Simon's preaching. Behind the "broadside against the religious" stands the denunciation of the logic of sacrifice, the hard core of the religious. Louis Simon discerns, beginning with the composition of the enigmatic episode of the binding of Isaac in the book of Genesis, the possibility of a non-sacrificial reading, precisely in the spirit of the gift of the indigent widow, a reading which would be covered over by an interpretation conforming to the sacrificial theology common to all the religions. Two commentaries on the Gospel articulate this denunciation, or to say it better, the renunciation of the interpretation of the cross of Jesus which has dominated for two millennia of Christian theology. First is the narrative of the tearing of the Temple curtain at the moment of the Crucifixion, which is audaciously interpreted as "the end of religious organizations." Simon arrives at this interpretation by means of a confrontation between two places, namely, the Temple as sacred place and Golgotha as the place of ritual murder, having become a cursed place, the place of life given. The second text, actually the last one of the collection, deals with the passage in Mark about the empty tomb, leaving aside the conclusion added by the final redactors. There is no marvel of appearances, but simply a disappeared body so that it is impossible to have him a little longer. Upon reading this narrative of absence, the parables of the absent master, the scenes of badgering, controversy, and rupture, in hind sight make Jesus' life look like a "slow disappearance." And in Galilee the Resurrected One is met only among the poor and excluded, the little people and the forgotten. In that way, he goes ahead of us. Louis Simon says, "He has disappeared; go, then, all of you, to seek him." The implicit theology of this group of sermons turns entirely on what I call a much stripped down reading of the Gospel. The total rupture with religion, sacrifice, and sacred place places the author very close to the René Girard of *Violence and the Sacred*. The sacrifice on the cross, understood as a gift of destitution, would mean the end of the logic of sacrifice, its total destruction.

I don't want to conclude this expression of profound agreement without giving voice to what I would call a note of perplexity. At the end of the century are we in a time when the opposition between the Gospel and religion can still be understood? I mean precisely this end of century and in the short term. Is the Gospel really so strongly menaced by the "pious"? Hasn't faith lost its vis-à-vis, religion? At the level of culture, the opposition faith-religion doesn't seem to work because there is scarcely much religion to dismantle.

I will pursue my question by following two convergent lines. First, looking from the outside, that is, from sociology of religion or more generally cultural facts, the vis-à-vis of radical Christian preaching is not the religion of the "pious" insiders. Rather it is from either what is left of what Raymond Aron calls the great secular religions of the mid-twentieth century, Hitlerism and Stalinism, or from the profane behavior of radically secularized societies that have been given over to what Max Weber, following Marcel Gauchet, calls "the disenchantment of the world." These societies no longer have the means to distinguish the Gospel from the "religiousness" denounced in this book. They tend to erase the traces of what falls under the words "religion," "sacrifice," and "sacred." They no longer pay attention to such detail.

Second, looking from inside the circle of evangelical preaching, the question arises whether this preaching can be understood without a connection to cult, liturgy, and ritual, which would ineluctably, whether one wishes it or not, classify expressions of faith with religious signs. At this point, the inside perspective joins the outside one: at a time when the total profanity of the world deprives faith of its anchor points, its means of access, must preaching not give rise to expectations and questions as much as put down pretentions and false responses? To do so, mustn't it make a selection among signs of the sacred while dissociating from the logic of sacrifice and religious moralism? What is put in question here is the place of Christian preaching within the general culture.

All the more, this question cannot be avoided because public discourse in profane society also often is about the poor, the excluded, and the forgotten of history. How can preaching understand its distinctness while joining with the best of profane discourse? Preaching exposes itself to this kind of questioning if it pushes the sheep "outside the pen."

Now that I have revealed this embarrassment I am tempted to say that it is necessary to pursue two types of discourse simultaneously. One in the short term and another for the long term. The first is that of the sociology of culture that asks about the present conditions for the communication of the Gospel, that is, how the discourse of faith connects with the outside. The second is the discourse of the long term, or rather of "contemporaneity" with the Jesus of the Gospels, necessarily interpreted with the resources of a specific culture. This discourse remains, Louis Simon has convinced me, a discourse of rupture, conformed to the extravagance of the parables, with an exception made for the festive moments which must not be forgotten. This latter discourse of contemporaneity cannot avoid implying a radical critique of the short-term cultural discourse. Simply, it credits the presumed inexhaustible capacity of the parable to speak with the grain and against the grain. For my part, I know of no expedient capable of harmonizing these two discourses.

—Paul Ricoeur

Preface

I say "my" Jesus, not out of pride, but with humility. For I know well that this Jesus is not the Jesus of everyone, and moreover, that it is not a question of imposing it on anyone. This Jesus is not the Jesus of the historians or the scholars, neither the Jesus of the ecclesiastical hierarchies and other guardians of "theological correctness." This Jesus is mine and, thus, partial and partisan. He is in my image because he gives me life and because he lives totally in me. He certainly is disputable and impertinent, but this Jesus is mine and I live from him.

But neither do I say "my" Jesus with a kind of possessive appetite that would give me property rights to an image or a beloved being, as if it were a thing at my disposition. No. To the contrary. It is Jesus who possesses me, haunts me, inhabits me. I am his companion only because he wants it that way. He would love to go with me everywhere and to do that he gives me signals, contradicts me and astonishes me. He follows me and precedes me. He is part of my history as I am of his. It is he who makes me love, think, and hope, from life to death. It is I who will speak of him. And not at all objectively, but subjectively. Like it is with all true passion. And finally (who knows?), like in all authentic witness.

N.B. Some of these texts have already been published in regional or national "Protestant" journals or preached on the radio. Many others have been heard only in the parishes where I have ministered. They are not arranged logically because they are made to be read one by one, in small doses! The text entitled *Zechariah* is the only one where it is not directly a question of "my" Jesus, but only of the people who waited for him. That of *Christ is Born in Pagan Territory* has become, through the argument developed, more a biblical study than a simple sermon.

Translator's Note - I am grateful to many people for their encouragement and help including, especially, Louis Simon, Colette Galland, Melissa Nickerson, Lynnette Fuller, Sue Ellen LaBelle, Bill Stroker, and the members of the Harvard Divinity School Alumni Discussion Group.

—CC

1

Two Unfinished Parables: The Treasure and the Pearl

Matthew 13:44–46

> *"The kingdom of heaven is like treasure hidden in a field, which someone found and hid; then in his joy he goes and sells all that he has and buys that field.*
>
> *"Again, the kingdom of heaven is like a merchant in search of fine pearls; on finding one pearl of great value, he went and sold all that he had and bought it."* NRSV

Here are two parables of the Kingdom of Heaven. I say "Kingdom of Heaven" to speak like Matthew, but for me that means: to have one day encountered Jesus of Nazareth and then done everything to remain close to him. For me, that's what the kingdom is: the very real way Jesus has of connecting with someone, and if possible forever.

These two parables form a pair. Many see them as similar, but in reality they describe two complementary aspects of the same good news.

If asked for the major idea common to these two parables one would have to say: it is a matter of an absolute adventure that requires absolute self-examination and renunciation.

It is true that it is a matter of losing all in order to receive all, to sell all in order to obtain all. A careful reading of these texts will show that it is an unreasonable adventure, frankly, pure folly.

It is indeed folly to renounce all that one has, sees, possesses, and lives on to get a treasure or pearl which in one sense is absurdly useless! Since one can live off of this treasure or pearl only to the extent that one draws from them and uses them up, uses them and destroys them. One cannot live without spending these priceless goods. One cannot eat by simply contemplating them. It is folly to suddenly find oneself empty, without resources, alone and with no means of existence, gazing at this absurd treasure and pearl! For these words have just one meaning: to sell all is to sell all. What folly to find oneself one day completely bereft and naked holding a pearl . . .

This folly is extreme because it reveals to us an *impossible alternative*: to die but keeping intact the treasure or to live by spending the treasure or selling the pearl, thereby losing them once again!

What loss of balance, this passion for the Kingdom. Everything comes down to this: live by losing the object of our passion or die by keeping it. That's what the strange gospel of these two parables wants to say to us.

Let's look now at what each of them says, separately, beginning with the Pearl. Usually we call it the Parable of the Pearl of Great Price. But actually it is a parable of a *merchant*. Here the Kingdom is not like a hidden treasure, but like a man who searches, a merchant who goes all over in search of a pearl that he wants to acquire. I like this touch: the Kingdom is first of all *someone* who searches, because then we can say that Jesus of Nazareth is like a pearl merchant who, having found a pearl of great price, goes and sells everything, all that he has, and buys it.

The absurdity of the fatal passion (this death necessary for the Kingdom) is supported by the Nazarene. He is the rich merchant who consents to be stripped of all his glory in order to possess the pearl that he has discovered. He lowers himself and is humiliated, he divests and empties himself to acquire this marvelous pearl. He is the Son of Man come to find the priceless stone, beloved of God, the capstone of creation, a human being, all humans, me.

The Kingdom of Heaven is revealed only there, in that disaster, that fatal emptying of the Cross on Good Friday.

Now we can consider the other parable, that of the *Treasure*. It is the same gospel but this time the focus is on humans, the object of the passion of the merchant. Here as well we have the characteristic severe stripping away, but perhaps also the fact of a strange *discovery*. Nested in the parable is the unusual, surprising touch which reveals the ways of the Kingdom which are not our ways.

Here we have an unknown, an anonymous man, indistinguishable from others, who does only what everyone else does. He works in a field digging with a shovel the same as countless others that day. We have an ordinary man who does nothing extraordinary. He has already done thousands of times, perhaps during thousands of days, this banal labor, this work of man. And then, all of a sudden something unusual . . .

By chance with a stroke of the shovel, a very ordinary push, a thrust of the shovel not prepared, not contrived, not researched, not pious . . . by chance from a stroke of the shovel, the Kingdom! The Kingdom is there, at his feet. The Kingdom fallen from the sky. Why him? Why not someone else? On what basis did he merit this strike from heaven? The Kingdom is the unexpected: gratuitous election, unmerited choice. You are the one for whom I reserve my Treasure . . .

There is the secret of the Kingdom. You are the one who has cost so much, who has counted for so much in the story of the Nazarene. You were chosen, by grace, so that you could discover today under the clods of wet clay, under the banality of the everydayness of your life, this great treasure of your election.

This is the mystery: the Treasure that I find there, without warning, terrible and splendid like a bolt of lightning from the sky is that I am, *me* (why me?), the one that the Nazarene has looked so hard for, and loved so much.

The Treasure that I find is that I am the Pearl.

Is this strange blessing, egoistic and unhealthy, the Kingdom of Jesus? I am overwhelmed, bursting at the seams, rich beyond counting. I need nothing, nor no one

. . . Ouch! *Where is the mistake?* What in my reading of the text led to this derangement?

But in reality wasn't this treasure fraudulently confiscated by its finder, stolen *for himself alone?*

This pearl, would it not be even more beautiful if it remained always attached with *many others*, in a marvelous necklace?

Two unfinished parables: it remains for me to discover in my life how Jesus himself will lead me *to complete his two parables.* For, in his Kingdom, I am absolutely certain that *I am nothing without the others!*

Nothing, without the others.

2

The Companions of Jesus

LUKE 14:16–24

Then Jesus said to him, "Someone gave a great dinner and invited many. At the time for the dinner he sent his slave to say to those who had been invited, 'Come; for everything is ready now.' But they all alike began to make excuses. The first said to him, 'I have bought a piece of land, and I must go out and see it; please accept my regrets.' Another said, 'I have bought five yoke of oxen, and I am going to try them out; please accept my regrets.' Another said, 'I have just been married, and therefore I cannot come.' So the slave returned and reported this to his master. Then the owner of the house became angry and said to his slave, 'Go out at once into the streets and lanes of the town and bring in the poor, the crippled, the blind, and the lame.' And the slave said, 'Sir, what you ordered has been done, and there is still room.' And the master said to the slave, 'Go out into the roads and lanes, and compel people to come in, so that my house may be filled. For I tell you, none of those who were invited will taste my dinner.'" NRSV

WE MUST not forget that most of the time when Jesus spoke he was backed into a corner, faced with enemies eager to defeat him.

Very quickly he—a simple lay person—found all the theologians lined up against him. Very quickly he—a worker scarcely thirty years old from a small village in the North—had all the elders and wise men of the capital against him. Things were going badly after just a few months. Every day brought a new drama, and he was worn out; it was a perpetual trial. They set trap after trap for him. They seized on everything he said. They tried to push him into errors. They tried to trick him. It was a real witch hunt, with a condemnation to death on the horizon.

We must also never forget that this man, who wanted only love, forgiveness, and tenderness, was obliged to debate, defend himself, bite his tongue, and cry out against his enemies who were stronger and better placed than himself. He lived with a suspended death sentence. That is the Jesus who speaks. You would think that his words would have the bitter taste of a harassed man, tormented by fear, that his speech would quaver, lack confidence, come sadly from a mouth dry with anguish. But he does not speak that way, this thirty-year-old man who does not wish to be *already dead*.

All of that is amplified when we see him among his strange entourage. What credit can be given to a man surrounded with such a shady bunch? We can understand the poor and the beggars; but the others? The deformed, the lepers, the epileptics, the sick, the unclean, and of course the sinners and unforgiven who have not given even the least required sacrifice in the Temple. And this is not to mention the collaborators, prostitutes, and Samaritans. Jesus' closeness with the poor and outsiders, the little people and the heretics, the disrespected and the immigrants, all of them together following him, is what sunk him.

And he knew this. *He wanted it that way.* To the end, Jesus preferred his compromising solidarity with the losers and the rejected to the esteem of the notables. He made his choice in full knowledge of what he was doing; intimacy with the weak is worth more than the flattery of the important people! Since the privileged invitees refused the invitation, God invited the excluded instead! Jesus declared, that is my God, the unconditional friend of the forgotten ones, even the sinners! Scandalous? *Yes.* And he deliberately added fuel to the fire by concluding: since all of you have scorned the invitation to my Master's festival, I have made my choice. Even if it costs me my life, I am and will remain with these strange neighbors. My God is the God of the little ones and the poor!

My friend, tell me where these curious companions of Jesus are today. Did Jesus speak for nothing? Did he die for nothing after all? Where can we find this astonishing bunch that he stood with so strongly? Are they in our homes, our chapels, our churches? Tell me, my friend, where must I go to find him today? *Will Jesus be among his friends?*

O Jesus, my brother, king without subjects, prophet without followers, we have changed your entourage! Around you now are the rich and well-regarded. Have you changed your mind? Have you given in to the pressure?

Or perhaps you have silently departed and gone on the road to be among the brothers and sisters you have always had. And I have permission to join you, to serve and love you. O Jesus, my brother.

3

Did Jesus Speak with Authority?

MARK 1:21–28

They went to Capernaum; and when the Sabbath came, he entered the synagogue and taught. They were astounded at his teaching, for he taught them as one who had authority, and not as the scribes. Just then there was in their synagogue a man with an unclean spirit, and he cried out, "What have you to do with us, Jesus of Nazareth? Have you come to destroy us? I know who you are, the Holy One of God." But Jesus rebuked him, saying, "Be silent, and come out of him!" And the unclean spirit, convulsing him and crying with a loud voice, came out of him. They were all amazed, and they kept on asking one another, "What is this? A new teaching--with authority! He commands even the unclean spirits, and they obey him." At once his fame began to spread throughout the surrounding region of Galilee. NRSV

Did Jesus Speak with Authority?

Did Jesus speak with authority? Apparently, this is a needless question since the Gospel gives us a clear response: Yes, "he speaks with authority, and not as the scribes!"

This took place in Capernaum on a Sabbath day when Jesus spoke publicly for the first tine: a memorable event.

But I am disturbed by this episode in Capernaum. The service is underway—prayers, readings from the Law and portions from the prophetic books in both Hebrew and Aramean so that everyone could understand. Pharisees provide commentary on the texts, and Jesus as well, but for him it is the first time he has spoken in a synagogue. His first sermon. The ritual of his entry into ministry. Thus, a very important moment.

And suddenly there is a great hubbub unlike anything seen before. A sick person begins to shout; actually it is a demon speaking through his mouth. "Jesus of Nazareth . . . you are the Holy One of God," the Son of God, the One sent from God. And this unexpected cry grabs everyone's attention. And it gets my attention, too, because this demon speaks like my church in its hymns . . .

But Jesus experiences this as an unacceptable aggression. A battle begins between Jesus and this speech from the other. A tumult. Peremptory exchanges. Rebukes. Loud cries. What a scandal! Never has this been seen at a service. The crowd is engaged. Jesus makes a decisive strike. There is a conqueror and a conquered. A good fight. No, says Mark, not a good fight; rather, a teaching, a *teaching having "authority."* And, with that, I am having difficulty figuring it out . . .

Would that be Jesus' teaching: confrontation without mercy?

This is an important question, because Jesus' teaching is the whole of Jesus. Absolutely all. It is the Gospel. It is my point of reference, that to which I consecrate my life. Loving Jesus consists in desiring to live his teaching.

One thing at first throws me off, but finally I understand. We do not know at all what Jesus said! Not a word. Teaching, OK, but *what*? We know nothing of it. That makes one think.

The authority of Jesus' teaching does not at all come from what is said (of that, we know nothing), but rather from elsewhere, from *him* perhaps, from who he is when he speaks (leave aside the content of what he said), from what is produced when he rises to speak, from the *speech event* which occurs, from this coming to us of a new word which is called Word, Word of God. The arrival of God among us, in speech.

A Word without fixed content, without image. A Word which is the real presence of God among us and for us.

He spoke, and the world began anew. And everyone began anew who was visited, inhabited, invested with this Word which changed all things. The Word was not in what was said but in this creation of new life, this apparition of life, this life where each one became new, different in oneself and different as partner of the other.

In truth, authority is that: the capacity to be an author. The author gives birth, makes something begin. Like a father and mother who bring a child into the world. Father and mother, agents of my beginning, are therefore authority for me.

When Jesus spoke, he was this kind of creator. If, unfortunately, he had written, his word would be reduced to a content. But he spoke, and he is the author of a new world. He created around him a new humanity, a kingdom. He spoke, and I began. It is a Word that gives birth not to slaves obliged to reproduce an imposed model from a dictated content, but kings, inventors of new worlds, poets of words still to come.

Yes, Jesus is this Word which is Author, Authority, and it is this Word which has *authorized* me, yes me, to be freely me, king with him in his kingdom and in mine. He taught them as a man who is authority.

But I must go back to the synagogue because in fact, and contrary to appearances, things did not go as well as I have said. I am remembering what Luke has the Devil say in the narrative of the temptation of Jesus: "All power has been given to me, and I give it to whom I will!"[1] So, all power is diabolical! I am distinguishing here between the *power* of the Devil and the *authority* of Jesus. But that is to have mercy on you, because in reality it is the same word in both cases.

We must face up to this unacceptable discovery: we don't yet know who speaks with authority, Jesus or the Devil.

Let's try to get clear. I called Jesus' authority the beginning of new life, a creation of community and finally of union. In opposition, I have the sense that diabolical power justifies and perpetuates not union but radical inequality that engenders a relation between forces, a violence which

1. Luke 4:6.

is brutal (or polite). Consequently, power needs only slaves—voluntary (or involuntary), happy (or in revolt). Power fears only free persons.

What happened in the synagogue? I see that Jesus rebukes (vs. 25), commands (vs. 27), launches orders without reply that provoke fear, submission and obedience (vs. 27). Is this breaking in a stubborn animal? Is it dialogue? Not in the least. "Silence, be quiet!," says Jesus (vs. 25) and whomever resists is thrown to the ground. Yes, a session of breaking in, a meeting of forces, a flagrant inequality, a terribly effective brutality—a *power*! At the synagogue of Capernaum we have a conqueror and a conquered.

But who is conquered?

Now here is how I have come to understand what Mark wants to say to me in his Gospel: I *myself* am this synagogue, this place where words are in crisis. I have taken Jesus into my life so that he can speak to me about Scripture. And he has done so, often. And I am completely incapable of telling you what he has taught me. Even at my deepest level, I listen to him without understanding. This is because I have *two* words in me. Because I understand only what I want to understand. Because I am religious, go to service and never miss a Sabbath. Because I sing, "Jesus, I know who you are, you are the Holy One of God!" Because what I want is to follow a Jesus full of power, a true Zorro. Because I want to be a slave of the All-Powerful, to be the domestic puppy of a Lord of Heaven and Earth, a dog who gets his sugar cube when he is good and says his prayers. Power.

Yes, I have two words in me. With all my force I smother the word which frees me, that of *Authority*, that which would authorize me, which would authorize my life, would give me the right to simply be who I am. For I do not love freedom. I don't want someone to let go of my hand. No, I do not like to walk alone, freely. It's too tiring. It wears me out. I'm too exposed. Too adult. Yes, that is who I am: a true Capernaum.

Jesus speaks, speaks, speaks in all the corners of my life. And I don't listen. I want to grab only the crumbs of his *Power*, even among the dogs, under the table. I am inhabited by this impure spirit. Religious by desire, I speak willingly of Jesus, the Holy One of God, but am a slave, a parasite attached to the All-Power of my idol.

But here is today's Gospel: "He teaches as one having authority." He has delivered me from my fear of being free . . .

Certainly it is not easy to "begin," to be placed in the world. But now *he authorizes me!*

I have met the author of my life. I now want to abandon the old order. I want to be a thinker of the disorder of life, poet of mobility, and following him, daring passionate incertitudes. . .

4

Pamphlet Against the Pious

Luke 10:29–37

But wanting to justify himself, he [a lawyer], asked Jesus, "And who is my neighbor?" Jesus replied, "A man was going down from Jerusalem to Jericho, and fell into the hands of robbers, who stripped him, beat him, and went, away, leaving him half dead. Now by chance a priest was going down that road; and when he saw him, he passed by on the other side. So likewise a Levite, when he came to the place and saw him, passed by on the other side. But a Samaritan while traveling came near him; and when he saw him, he was moved with pity. He went to him and bandaged his wounds, having poured oil and wine on them. Then he put him on his own animal, brought him to an inn, and took care of him. The next day he took out two denarii, gave them to the innkeeper, and said, 'Take care of him; and when I come back, I will repay you whatever more you spend.' Which of these three, do you think, was neighbor to the man who fell into the hands of the robbers?" He said, "The one who showed him mercy." Jesus said to him, "Go and do likewise." NRSV

Is THERE a passage in the Gospel harder for clergy than this one? It begins by (nearly) killing someone. I confess, it kills me. And it wants to do the same to you this morning. Only at the end of the reading, the very end, is one resuscitated by consenting to be at the unconditional service of others. But the only one brought back to life is the one who has agreed to be placed in the line of fire of the implacable Word of Jesus.

This Parable of the Good Samaritan must be re-read as it wants to be read, namely, a pamphlet against the pious. All the details are fitting for a pamphlet. There are the caricatures of two representatives of religion who are outrageously indefensible. And of course opposite them is the provocative choice of the hereditary enemy—the Samaritan—to play the good guy. There is no way out, for the dice are loaded . . . How can we make a case for the religious types?

We also have an unlikely situation, invented by Luke, where a doctor of the Law, that is to say, an expert and a professor of theology, consults a layperson, Jesus, on an interpretation of the Law. To set it up so that the professors of Israel are reduced to being instructed by the laity is an anticlerical attitude that already casts the text in the form of a pamphlet. And then, above all, we have the finale of a childish riddle. The doctor of Law would have expected something more serious such as a learned exposition leading to some subtle *distinguo*. But instead of that the doctor is told an impossible little story in which the roles are fixed and the choice is between a priest and Levite who do nothing and a Samaritan who does everything, and more than everything! It is too simple. Any child would agree. You are making fun of the doctors of the Law when you imagine them incapable of seeing the difference (as, moreover, did Matthew) between a mosquito and a camel, between a Levite and some Samaritan! The final riddle is also pamphlet-like. What could one hope for from religious experts who do not know how to sort out the evidence, who would filter mosquitoes out of their drink but continue to swallow camels?

Yes, a gospel pamphlet against the clergy and the pious. And, consequently, against *me*.

The narrative has three characteristics that propose a triple attack against my self-sufficiency.

First information (which hurts me): by wanting to be sure of communion with God, the religious person *loses the neighbor*.

According to Jesus, this is literally what happens to the priest and the Levite. And this is the first original feature of the narrative.

Two pious men are going up to Jerusalem, that is, going toward the Temple to perform their religious function. Since the wounded man at the side of the road is "half-dead," they absolutely must avoid him. So they pass by on the other side in order to put the maximum distance between themselves and the probable dead man. For proximity to the dead means contamination. And if they come to Jerusalem unclean they will not be able to be in the service of God for seven days. They turn away from the wounded man not because they are mean or insensitive, but because they are *good religious people*, faithful to the Levitical rules. And this is what touches me about the first point: the more scrupulous you are about religious matters the less you can risk serving the profane and the unclean. The more you wish to keep your hands clean the less you will have hands. And we all know that it is the best religious people in our societies who risk letting the wounded die on our roads!

The second characteristic is the word "neighbor." And here is where I am openly denounced. Religious people call "neighbors" only those who are *like them*.

This time, clergy or not, we are all targeted. We, like Israel, readily agree that it is right to serve neighbors, but what we refuse is to extend the quality of neighbor to just anyone.

We are fiercely egoistic. We truly love only ourselves. At best, we can love those who resemble us, that is, those in whom we can find a reflection of ourselves! To love co-religionists, for example, is still a little bit to love oneself. Love among similars can lead to a kind of principle of connected vessels whereby everything is redistributed to everyone. And the love that one puts in (who knows?) could come back increased. But here, with the figure of the Samaritan, Jesus whacks all the religious types. Jesus says that the neighbor is the other, the different one, the one that you reject, the one outside, the stranger.

My neighbor is the one that I regard as my enemy! Who can accept that? The second pamphlet lesson says to me: pay attention, my friend, for the more religious you are and the more you are convinced of what of you believe, the more you risk loving only yourself, consequently dying.

Ultimate attack, last wound: the pious end up living in an unreal world, cut off from life and deprived of all knowledge!

Do I exaggerate?

The theologian in the parable behaves like a fool who has lost his senses. The context underlines this. Jesus asked him to recite out loud the summary of the Law: you must love God and your neighbor. And the theologian—this is monstrous when we think about it—*knows* God whom he does not see but hesitates about neighbors with whom he deals every day! We could have understood if he had said, But where is God? or Where can I encounter God so as to love God? No. The sole thing that perturbs him is this: Where can I find a neighbor?

A foolish man who *cuts himself off from reality*, from real people. A sick man who takes refuge in the imaginary, a world of invisible things. He is sure of only what no one can see. He is perplexed only by what is before his very eyes. He is an alienated man who inhabits a shadow world, a chimera!

This ultimate attack wounds me to the death. Those who know God better than neighbor know nothing. They are no longer human, but delirious and tragically disconnected from reality. My friend, the more you wish to live in heaven the more you will become evil on earth!

There I am, wounded and half-dead. Now who is going to come to help me? Who will be my neighbor?

He comes toward us. He sees us, comforts us, heals us. We, who are to him so "other," so much the enemy. And at the end of the story, he is there, at our side, to say to us: I am there, and now, *you*, go and do likewise!

5

Zacchaeus Climbs a Tree

Luke 19:1–10

He entered Jericho and was passing through it. A man was there named Zacchaeus; he was a chief tax collector and was rich. He was trying to see who Jesus was, but on account of the crowd could not, because he was short in stature. So he ran ahead and climbed a sycamore tree to see him, because he was going to pass that way. When Jesus came to the place, he looked up and said to him, "Zacchaeus, hurry and come down; for I must stay at your house today." So he hurried down and was happy to welcome him. All who saw it began to grumble and said, "He has gone to be the guest of one who is a sinner." Zacchaeus stood there and said to the Lord, "Look, half of my possessions, Lord, I will give to the poor; and if I have defrauded anyone of anything, I will pay back four times as much." Then Jesus said to him, "Today salvation has come to this house, because he too is a son of Abraham. "For the Son of Man came to seek out and to save the lost." NRSV

Zacchaeus Climbs a Tree

THE SCENE takes place in Jericho, city of great decisive battles. Already this setting leads us to suspect that the new Joshua of Nazareth will once again make walls tumble down, walls of wealth and of religion.

Zacchaeus; the name is almost a symbol. He has chosen to become fraudulently rich by becoming chief tax collector for Jericho; that is, he made a pact with the Roman occupier and thereby was excluded from the synagogue. His connection to Israel was still present through his name which recalls the demand to obey God (Zacchaeus means "the Pure One"). Therein lies the drama concerning this man; he is pure but knows that he is impure. The whole world calls him Zacchaeus (the Pure One). But regards him as a deliberate sinner, obstinate, and ostentatious, for a chief tax collector is a little like chief sinner.

This sad contradiction secretly eats away at Zacchaeus. It makes him guilty without recourse, remorseful without relief, a sad sinner. Moreover, he is physically one of the smallest men in Jericho, yet lives in the style of the greatest! He is alienated and ripe for religion. But it is precisely this religious need that closes him in and feeds his malaise. He is too Jewish and religious to be a tranquil sinner and too much a sinner to be tranquilly religious.

Jesus appears. Nearly everyone takes him to be the Messiah. And for all Jews the Messiah would be the implacable adversary of the Roman collaborators. Thus, Zacchaeus said to himself: here is my judge. And since Jesus had said terrible things against the rich, Zacchaeus said for a second time: here is my judge.

And now begins *the triumph of religion*. Zacchaeus runs ahead *to climb* a sycamore tree. He said to himself, at least I will be great in my smallness and my public confession of my pettiness will be grand. I chose to be great and notable, so now I will grandly attest that I am notably ridiculous. To the exploit of being rich, Zacchaeus now replies with the exploit of being contemptible. That's the way it is with pious people made guilty by their religion: always too much! They are too rich in their sins and also too rich in confession of their faults. Zacchaeus must have been truly sick to choose to punish himself publicly this way, to run to meet his judge instead of closing his doors and windows, and to advertise himself so theatrically as an extraordinary and unexpected penitent.

Zacchaeus had had enough of his official identity, that of the sinner banished from Israel. But he casts aside one identity to put on another! And what an identity, one more eloquent and amusing than the other! . . . Ever after, Zacchaeus will be the tax collector who climbs trees to punish himself, exposes himself to the crowd's mockery (at least he thinks so), in order to be seen by the Messiah who is coming and will bring an end to history and proceed to the Last Judgment.

Zacchaeus is the first monk, the inventor of self-punishment. Of course, Simeon the Stylite will do it better by perching for years on a column. But Zacchaeus launches the movement! He seeks justice through columns and trees, where one is dressed not in one's justice, but in one's injustice.

Jesus appears, and with him the entire content of the Gospel in a single command: "Zacchaeus, hurry and come down!"

Come down quickly. The new life is not one of rising but a way of descending; not a way of escaping the everyday, but of inserting oneself into the everyday. The Gospel is not above the fray, above the crowds, beyond taxes. It is an engagement with the crowd in behalf of a better system of taxes.

Come down quickly, says Jesus. Stop being a religious monkey in your tree. I am not in the trees. You don't meet me somewhere between heaven and earth. I am down below, in the midst of the crowd, among people. To live my Gospel you do not soar above the ground; rather, you bury yourself in it like a seed which must mature so that it can reap a harvest of ten-, fifty-, and even one hundred-fold.

Come down quickly! God isn't found on high. God lives at root level. Stop being a monk-monkey and become a man!

Jesus appears, and with him the whole Gospel: "Zacchaeus, I must stay at your house today." There is the true conversion of Zacchaeus. He doesn't need to flee his house; he needs to learn that it is one of the houses of Jesus.

My house, says Jesus, is not the Temple, nor the Synagogue, nor the Church, nor the sky, nor the trees. My house is *your* house with its dishonest transactions. There, together, we are going to plant the seed of the greatest economic revolution that Jericho could know: restore fourfold what has been falsely gained and give half to the poor. The conversion of Zacchaeus happens neither in heaven nor in a tree, but in his house. He must make his house into a sign of the Kingdom. It is where he is as he is, with what he has that he will become a disciple of the Son of Man.

How can this be? How can we recognize that this miracle of Jericho took place? This way. Zacchaeus will exchange the false anguish of a personal justice for a better justice *for others*. For sure, he is not worry free (to the contrary, his true worries are about to begin), but he has left religion for the Gospel. He is about to discover the primacy of others, particularly the primacy of the poor. That is the Gospel.

It is not only Jesus who has just entered his house; with him have come all the poor. Without the poor, everything is false, especially the famous word of Zacchaeus: "I will give half of my possessions to the poor." For if the accent is not on the poor but remains attached to the I, it would be just another way of Zacchaeus climbing a tree . . .

But now he no longer says I; he says "the poor . . ." He will seek *only* the justice of the Kingdom, which at this moment takes the form of a better justice for Jericho. Zacchaeus know that on top of it all, all will be given to him, starting with his joy over living beside the Son of Man.

This was Jericho. The walls came tumbling down! A rich religious man became a prophet of the Gospel. Immediately, at the heart of his city and the ambiguity of human history, he began the construction of a world as a parable of the Kingdom.

To construct a world as a parable of the Kingdom!

6

The Temptation to Do Good

MARK 1:40–45

A leper came to him begging him, and kneeling he said to him, "If you choose, you can make me clean." Moved with pity, Jesus stretched out his hand and touched him, and said to him, "I do choose. Be made clean!" Immediately the leprosy left him, and he was made clean. After sternly warning him he sent him away at once, saying to him, "See that you say nothing to anyone; but go, show yourself to the priest, and offer for your cleansing what Moses commanded, as a testimony to them." But he went out and began to proclaim it freely, and to spread the word, so that Jesus could no longer go into a town openly, but stayed out in the country; and people came to him from every quarter. NRSV

I CONFESS to you that I do not like miracles. It's not that I don't believe in them! No. I am totally convinced that Jesus performed many healings, and thanks to him, the crowds of desperate people found hope for their bodies and meaning for their lives. Here is what upsets me. Each time that I read an account of healing, behind the act of healing I hear a terrible determination of Jesus. By choosing to heal others he accepts to die. And that hurts me.

The healing of *a leper*, such as we have here, is exemplary. For everything happens as prescribed by the book of Leviticus. *Two birds* are taken to the priest. One is sacrificed and its blood is sprinkled on the other which is set free toward the sky, toward life. One dead and one living, which is the situation with the healing of a leper. So that it will be clear, Jesus makes a specific reference to this sacrifice. "Go, show yourself to the priest, and offer for your cleansing what Moses has prescribed." Two birds: one dead, the other living healed and free. I tremble at each miracle because of this somber and tragic face, because of the dead bird. "Go, show yourself to the priest!" You can't joyously celebrate a healing of a leper without also hearing the doleful cry of the dead bird, its last cry. And also hear the "grumbling" of the only Son pushed to walk toward death and his last cry, "My God, my God, why . . . ?"

Friends, always remember that, yes, one bird is free, but there is also one dead bird.

Jesus is the Word, Jesus speaks. Speaking occurs when two or more persons inhabit a free space. Speakers hope for comprehension, a response, attention, a debate, even agreement, but in complete freedom. Without freedom there is no speaking. Without freedom the words die and become mere commands. *A miracle gives a signal.* It terrorizes and constrains the partner, subjugates, casts a spell, achieves seduction and total capitulation. The miracle is not speech. Understood properly, the miracle is the enemy of the word. For miracles function as signals and automatically gain admiration. By miracles one gains renown (renom) but loses one's name (nom).

Choosing to accept the way of the miracle, which indeed heals the sick, is choosing to become renowned, a personage, a hero created by the covetousness of others. It is to accept adulation because of the healing you perform. In the first chapter, the evangelist already noted: "His fame spread everywhere . . ." The drama is set. The crowds gather. How can they be refused a healing? Yes, the crowds hang on his coattails. They come to *see*, to have a spectacle. Line up here! But in fact they did not come to *understand*! Soon the brute sound of signs and wonders will have taken over, leaving no room for a free exchange of words.

Wasn't this also the meaning of the Temptation of Jesus narrative at the beginning of his ministry? Namely, it is the risk of losing the Word because of the success of the miracles and signs. Apparently miracles save time because they don't require much from the Word. However, by doing so they alienate rather than deliver, creating clients instead of awakening persons.

Thus the *shadow of Golgotha* gets a step closer with each miracle. Why give in to the crowds and the demons? Each time Jesus agrees to heal he loses a chance to offer the Word. To heal the other, for Jesus, is to kill a little more his own word and his proclamation of the Gospel. Alas! But to heal someone is a big thing! How can you refuse to heal? When he encounters suffering, Jesus, sorrowfully, chooses to heal at the price of his own word. Yes, two birds: one is free, but the other will die.

I am deeply touched to see how Mark the evangelist carefully notes the *internal debate* (which later Matthew and Luke don't dare to repeat). Only Mark speaks of Jesus' strong emotion in the face of suffering. Because of the emotion, Jesus concedes to perform the miracle. Only Mark reports this strange behavior (which upsets me): "He sternly charged him, and sent him away at once . . ." Why this violent move if not to underline the sad test that Jesus will have to endure? Yes, he *must* heal this man begging for help on his knees, but it is hard to realize that by doing so he crucifies his own word and life! . . . So, the sight of this healthy man whom one has freed and healed is intolerable, too much. "He sternly charged him, and sent him away . . ." It is a harsh verb; he expelled him. It is as if Jesus could no longer—all of a sudden—stand to see this happy face which condemned both him and his word.

Too much power wears out the word. Too many miracles get in the way of speaking person to person, at the human level. Jesus' renown imprisons him. He can no longer meet people face to face. He is a fabulous personage, placed higher, too high. And this is before he has been lifted up high, dominant, overwhelming, half-god, god . . . Alas.

A cry of distress sounds forth. A hand reaches out. A look implores. Such is the pathos of the miracle narratives. And it just drives nails into the hands of the Son. The leper begs: "If you will, you can . . ." Gethsemane: not what I will, but these little and needy ones do me in with their eyes dimmed with distress . . .

Sorrowful Son of Man. He is the Word, but he loves so much the poor and desolate that cross his path that, little by little, he tolerates the systematic destruction of the conditions of his word. The Son of Man truly takes on himself the sickness of others, all the way to death. He knows that he is being used. But, he wants it. He knows that he is being taken for someone he isn't, but he agrees to walk into that night if it means the healing of a single person. This is how he has chosen to live: *by dying*. He will let himself be taken and disrobed. In full lucidity, he will be had. He will accept being no more than a word buried in the ambiguity of healing actions . . .

Mark continues; he dares to record the whole *dramatic conclusion* of his story. After the outburst that tore him from the other, Jesus suddenly breaks down. He begs, he beseeches, he implores. He wants a delay, a reprieve. *If you please, say nothing to any one.* If you please, allow me to approach people as an unknown so that I can speak to them in complete freedom, without our relation being falsified beforehand . . . If you please . . . Give me a chance . . .

Mark brutally crucifies the Word by continuing without equivocation: "But he went out and began to talk freely about it, and to spread the news . . ."

So, it's all over. Jesus speaks, and things no longer happen. He has already lost his word. He has put on this personage that he did not want, and already it is killing him. Two birds: one set free, the other dead.

The death in question is his word. We must recapture it and live by it.

It was a leper. Now, a leper is always more than a leper. It is an entire society organized with exclusive places and excluded people. It is all the cities that park some people in the ghettos or special zones in order to protect the elites from their hunger for justice and humanity. It is on this side of town that I have heard some buried words of the Son of Man, who has not stopped dying there, wordlessly, for the freedom of the poor.

7

Is Leprosy Contagious?

Matthew 8:1–4

When Jesus had come down from the mountain, great crowds followed him; and there was a leper who came to him and knelt before him, saying, "Lord, if you choose, you can make me clean." He stretched out his hand and touched him, saying, "I do choose. Be made clean!" Immediately his leprosy was cleansed. Then Jesus said to him, "See that you say nothing to anyone; but go, show yourself to the priest, and offer the gift that Moses commanded, as a testimony to them." NRSV

MARK HAD already written the narrative of the healing of the leper. He organized it around Jesus, noting his emotions, his anxiety, his sternness, in short, his internal debate over whether the success of his miracles would make him lose his "word."

Matthew retells the story, but gives Jesus a completely other status. He puts it in the form of a surprising encounter:

the Pure with the Impure, the Saint and the Damned, the King and the Leper. Right away this encounter becomes upsetting. It shows that to *encounter* someone is truly an extraordinary adventure in which the two protagonists are reached, touched, even deformed. How does this concern us?

Obviously, we are no longer in the privileged situation of the Galilean contemporaries of Jesus. Nevertheless, even for them, the "encounter" was problematic. Mark emphasizes the difficulty. Did they encounter Jesus of Nazareth or the renown of a stupefying healer? Did they encounter the person or the personage? The ambiguity lies there. And since it appeared impossible to evade or erase the Personage, what was required to correct things so as to recover the real Person of the Nazarene?

For us, the situation is still more complicated because we can encounter him only through the gospel witnesses. These witnesses were written only because of Easter and in order to make known the final victory of the Son. Since they were touched by that final light—literally possessed by it—how could the biblical writers *not* clarify in advance all the memories of his earthly journey? They could not forget the end of the story when they recounted the beginning. How could they have? Their writing, consequently, was full of Personage, even when they tried their best to describe the Person.

Our concern, then, is to recover, if possible, the Nazarene, including the emotion and innocent surprise of a *first encounter.* And to do this even though we know the end of the Gospel which created our faith, our appetite for knowledge, and our need to encounter him.

Is the leper so contagious that he can *disfigure* the Person into a Personage and Scripture into a deforming mirror?

The crowds descend from the mountain. They follow him in a mass. They know Jesus, they love him, and they can't get enough of him. He is a splendid performer of miracles.

But, all of a sudden, from outside the crowd, a man appears. He walks from the other direction, not from behind, but coming to meet Jesus. He isn't following. He blocks the way. He falls to the ground on his knees, looks at Jesus, and speaks. He takes the initiative. He is in charge. He directs the action.

No one knows where he comes from, neither his name nor his home village. He bears on his face the secret of his identity. He is a leper. He doesn't fall into step with Jesus; rather, he stops him. He doesn't listen to Jesus, but gives him orders. Rather than receiving teaching, he teaches! He is not evangelized, he evangelizes! He doesn't reveal himself to himself (by listening to what he heard) but he speaks to Jesus in order to reveal Jesus to Jesus. *You, Jesus, you can, if you choose* . . . Yes, it is the leper who announces to Jesus the good news of Jesus: you, Jesus, you can if you choose! You can become Jesus!

The man is standing up straight, tall, free! Others call him a leper: I call him a king. Leprosy does not have this grandeur. We, like the crowds, live like clients, begging for favors with our little prayers. He gives to Jesus the good news of Jesus. He doesn't take; he offers. He is not poor; he is rich. He does not beg; he reveals. He doesn't strip a Lord; he robes him. He adorns Jesus, crowns him, and consecrates him. You are anointed; you are Christ. Jesus, you can, if you choose, become Jesus!

There is a *free man*. We act like fearful children seeking shelter and refuge from a great one. This man alone is adult. Like a king, he gives Jesus his mission and launches him into his ministry. He authorizes Jesus. He enthrones Jesus. You can if you will. Dare to become Jesus!

Suddenly everything is clear, and we see what was growing before our eyes all along. The miracle is underway! Without any fear of being stoned (and legally, that is what would have happened to him), the leper has royally and tranquilly left the enclosure where he had been parked. He did not approach Jesus crying (as he was required to do) "Impure! impure! . . . impure! . . ." No. I tell you, the miracle is underway! It just happened. The miracle is this man, free and outside the prisons of pure and impure, who dared to live without prohibitions and barriers. He has gone out of his enclosure. He has walked toward Jesus, toward the crowd. He has confronted them. He has calmly disobeyed his entire religious legacy. He has made use of legs officially paralyzed by society. He has met Jesus and spoken to him, and he has done this without precaution or undue politeness. In addition, and this is a second miracle, no one has taken their distance from him. Others have approached, have come near. He has neighbors again. His faith, his freedom, his royalty as a free man has rubbed off on the others. The miracle is that his freedom, not the leprosy, is contagious! It's an enormous miracle of the kingdom of God.

And by touching him with his hands Jesus also breaks the Law. The walls of religion crumble. And now it is necessary that everyone participate, for Jesus is either a transgressor or the son of Freedom.

The truth is that what is contagious is not leprosy but the freedom of faith. A sick man has become King. A Jesus has entered into his ministry. For everyone it is the festival of the beginnings of the Kingdom!

"See that *you say nothing to anyone*, but *go, show yourself to the priest* . . ." What? Does leprosy retake the upper hand? Where is freedom?

It doesn't bother me that he is sent to the priest. Things being what they are, that is normal in Israel. It is appropriate that the sick person, healed individually, must also be healed socially, so that he fully recovers his place in the city. Going to the priest makes official, and therefore authentic, his reentry into society.

What bothers me is the other part: *speak to no one about this!*

I understand very well that Jesus demands this silence so that the popularity of miracles would not overshadow his message. But what is incomprehensible to me is the behavior of the evangelist! For the evangelists, first among all, would only have had to be quiet and the affair would have ended! Why recount this episode that explicitly includes a request for silence? Isn't it first of all the redactor of the gospel who disobeys Jesus? This is an enigma of *Scripture*: it preserves the words of Jesus *and* violates them! It transmits *and* betrays. Scripture has caught leprosy!

Speak to no one. Scripture says, to no one. So Scripture itself has organized an extravagant disobedience of Jesus.

Now everyone can know what must not be told. How can we understand that?

Here we return to the difficulties mentioned at the beginning. First, how can Jesus' contemporaries encounter the Person if they must begin with the Personage? Second, how can we desacralize Scriptures which are bathed in the glory of Easter?

The answer is short and simple. It is necessary to have two free men, such as this leper and this evangelist. Yes, it requires the unexpected boldness of this prayer that dares, still today, to address Jesus in the way a King speaks to his prophet. And it requires the smile and amused humility of biblical writing, capable of committing some blunders, so as not to take itself too quickly for the Word of God.

To be adult before Jesus in order to approach him person to person, and to remain adult and free in the examination of Scripture: that is how to recover our health. It is how to become again "contemporary" with the Nazarene. It is the freedom of the Gospel that is contagious, not leprosy.

Do you truly believe that Jesus would have loved being treated as a Christian idol? For myself, I am sure that he would have preferred that I meet him on even ground, person to person . . .

As my brother!

8

Jesus the Provocateur

Mark 2:13–18a

Jesus went out again beside the sea; the whole crowd gathered around him, and he taught them. As he was walking along, he saw Levi son of Alphaeus sitting at the tax booth, and he said to him, "Follow me." And he got up and followed him. And as he sat at dinner in Levi's house, many tax collectors and sinners were also sitting with Jesus and his disciples--for there were many who followed him. When the scribes of the Pharisees saw that he was eating with sinners and tax collectors, they said to his disciples, "Why does he eat with tax collectors and sinners?" When Jesus heard this, he said to them, "Those who are well have no need of a physician, but those who are sick; I have come to call not the righteous, but sinners." Now John's disciples and the Pharisees were fasting. NRSV

I WONDER why Mark assembled so many provocative acts of Jesus at the very beginning of his ministry. To believe

Mark, Jesus threw so much fuel on the fire that the Cross was guaranteed from the outset.

Consider, for example, Chapter 2.

The *healing of the paralytic* is a first provocation. How could the scribes not call it blasphemy? For them it is clear that God alone can offer pardon, and sacrifice in the Temple is required. Why provoke the scribes and show so clearly that for Jesus trips to the Temple are useless, even ridiculous?

Next, after calling and recruiting Levi (Matthew)—we will come back to this—, why make a point of joining a banquet with the brotherhood of excommunicated tax collectors on the very day of an official fast? And you know what follows next. There is the double ostentatious and gratuitous violation of the Sabbath: simply for amusement to pluck a few heads of grain when it would be so easy to wait a few hours to do manual labor. That is Chapter 2 at the beginning of the ministry. Jesus attacks on all fronts. Boldly and publicly he discredits sacrifice, fasting, and the Sabbath.

How could he hope to continue without conflict? In any case, we must remind ourselves of this explosive and resolutely provocative context when we reread the narrative of the calling of Levi. There had to be very serious reasons, even grave ones, for such actions by Jesus that broke with the religion of Israel and inaugurated a Gospel.

Jesus did not seek to reform Israel; his original vision is much more radical. It is to reinvent humanity based on total solidarity in hope. Thus, everything that could inhibit solidarity is attacked.

Does it even need to be spelled out? In Jesus' time the tax collector was an abominable person par excellence.

For example, in the eyes of a Pharisee Levi sat not only in the tax office, but at the very heart of sin. The tax collector was a professional, salaried sinner, betraying God and his nation by working for occupying Rome. He was an atheist who took orders from a foreign power and lived as an enemy of Religion. The provocation was that Jesus wanted such people among his companions of hope and struggle. Consequently, in the Gospel's list of the Twelve Apostles there will be such an unrepentant sinner, chosen as such.

Thus, in what we could say is the original structure of the Church, Jesus wanted a rebel that others condemn and excommunicate. The Church is fundamentally a community of sinners and saints. Jesus himself calls not the righteous, but sinners. He is here not for the healthy, but for the sick. There is a provocation that will henceforth transgress all boundaries of the church. Jesus included only the excluded. Already, that pushes out all who want to install themselves there . . .

The Gospel of the Nazarene consists of signing up Levi (Matthew) for his apostolic college and celebrating by having a banquet with sinners. This first public meal would be the basis for the meaning of all the others, including his final meal, the Last Supper.

My Church, says Jesus, must be defined not by the list of right-thinking religious people, but by its acts of solidarity with the ungodly of the city.

But his provocation disturbed everyone. No doubt Levi himself wasn't comfortable around the severe, sober, and pious former disciples of John the Baptist.

And we shouldn't underestimate the extent of excitement when the Pharisees interrupt the festival of gluttons (with whom Jesus was quite comfortable). It is not easy for anyone to follow Jesus, neither from the right or left, nor for the pious or the politicians. He says: "I came to call not the healthy, but the sick . . ."

Yes, but *who feels sick?* For the religious types (Pharisees), it is clear; the practically incurable sick are the "worldly ones" and the sinners. But do the tax collectors, who are thereby condemned, think of themselves as sick? Not at all. They are happy. They are fit. They are quite healthy, thank you very much. For them, the sick are the sad, smooth, and resistant pious people, the skinny Baptists who deprive themselves of the joys of the table and the good life . . . So, who is sick? Who is called?

Here is the Gospel answer. Because, no matter who I am, I always suspect that others are sick, I have to confess that my Lord is only the Lord of the others. He came to call . . . *the other*!

Jesus is not an iconoclast and provocateur just for fun. He is creator of new life, of a new community of life. His new word is *solidarity.*

With this pluralist group of the Twelve Jesus invents a church cut to his pattern: Essene rigorists, scrupulous Pharisees, angry and violent zealots, notorious sinners, and those who for a long time have been turned off by everything . . . There, that is a Church. Not some religious pietists who disengage from worldly preoccupations. Nor political reformers who would use religion for their purposes. But it is a strange group where each one salutes the other as a privileged companion of the Master, where one becomes oneself only by abandoning their own security and renouncing their pet concerns, whether they be pietist or activist.

Only solidarity can free us. Jesus' true provocation is that he did not want to abandon any one. No one! He breaks only with the spirit of separation, purity, clan, and caste. He separates himself only from the "pure ones" who imagine themselves to be somebody all by themselves. He turns away only from the sectarians who want to be only with those like them.

We must live from now on knowing that only the "different ones" (and not the similars) can shape the silhouette of the Kingdom. Following Jesus, they proclaim a nearly unconditional solidarity with the rejected and excluded, no matter where they come from or who they are.

The Gospel of the Nazarene says that to be just is no longer to separate or distinguish oneself from others; rather, it is to live with them in a solidarity of hope which right away takes on the allure of festival, of joy, and even of feasting with the Son of Man.

A living dog is worth more than a dead lion, and a sinner with others is worth more than a righteous one without others. Jesus calls . . . the other!

May the day come when on your daily round someone will signal to you and say with the astonishing simplicity of a child: you, my friend, follow me.

And may that lead you toward the Son of Man.

9

A Festival of Birds

MARK 4:30–32

He also said, "With what can we compare the kingdom of God, or what parable shall we use for it? It is like a mustard seed, which, when sown upon the ground, is the smallest of all the seeds on earth; yet when it is sown it grows up and becomes the greatest of all shrubs, and puts forth large branches, so that the birds of the air can make nests in its shade." NRSV

I THINK that Mark, with this little *Parable of the Mustard Seed*, has no need of a *Christmas Story*. Everything is already celebrated there, beginning with the truly miraculous character of the birth of the plant. In fact, his readers see only mystery and amazement in the surging forth of the shoot after the burial and death of the seed. At Christmas time we should always reread the tale of the festival of the mustard seed and of the one whom it announces!

A Festival of Birds 45

I am delighted first of all in this story of the sown seed by the fact that there is no "sower" at all! Of course, later, Matthew and Luke will introduce a "sower," a sire, a father, a Joseph. But Mark is the poet of Christmas who has no need to explain or make credible. When he wrote there was yet no need to evoke a Joseph without seed or a Mary without sire. It sufficed to celebrate the seed, come from who knew where, with the aid of no man acting as the master of history, to salute the miraculous beginning of the Nazarene.

Could it be that Matthew and Luke were wrong to wish to "naturalize" the mystery, to make it more credible? In any case, one doesn't serve the festival of Christmas well by wrapping it up in a more convincing narrative. I prefer Mark: no sower! And his Gospel never introduces the figure of Joseph! Nor for that matter Joseph's absence! This is speaking of Christmas in the register of the parables. A little seed without sower: that is the beautiful marvel suitable for making us think (without having to say it) that Jesus is a Son who cannot be explained by any father of this world.

And what I also love is the ending: no matter what one says, there is no tree! (To be sure, Matthew and Luke add a final tree!) No, no tree. In Mark's parable, at the end, there is still only the seed; but now it has become a marvelous shelter for the nests of all the birds of the sky! When the seed grows, it is not to become a tree, huge and glorious like a cedar, imposing with all its majesty and strength. No. The seed remains a seed, a new seed, with branches. And it must be named only with reference to the multitude that finds in it shelter and life.

Tree: that name must not be said too quickly! No, we must say something that belongs to all the other lives that fly around the seed which has grown. The story of the growth of the seed would be nothing without these "others." Mark reminds us (Why haven't Matthew and Luke understood this?) that at the end of the story of the seed (that is, its resurrection) we must keep the same quality of discretion and amazement as at the beginning. We must never be too hasty to say too much, to be too precise, to be too convincing. No tree. At the end, the amazement must come only from the side of the birds! They alone show the beautiful new volume of the sown seed.

The final description of the sown seed (its resurrection) does not speak of a glory too high, too majestic, and too heavy to be supported by humans. No: the mustard becomes only a little shrub that wouldn't scare the vegetables! I am told it would measure about 5 feet 11 inches. So, a glory at the height of a person. Here is what the seed comes to, the goal of its growth: a festival of birds in its crown, at the height of a person, with its chirping in our ears and before our eyes.

I understand that Mark has not written a "birth story" nor did he have need of a "resurrection" narrative. No sower, no tree. At the end, *a festival of birds* speaks better than any other story of the miraculous continuation of the Son sown on the earth.

I admit to having been too hard on Luke. In fact, when he wrote his version of the story of the mustard seed he allowed himself a little correction that makes me very happy. Luke introduces a word not found elsewhere in the synoptic gospels, and which brings with it all the magic of the poems of the origin (of the genesis) of the world: *the garden*. With that change it is a matter of the mustard seed "thrown toward the garden" (Luke 13:19). A poem of hope. The "Garden" is no longer condemned. Once again a human being heads toward Eden. With the sowing of the seed the bolts which blocked the hope of a humanity reconciled with its Lord are already broken! Beginning with Christmas hope is in order: a new humanity is possible! Its history is relaunched toward the Garden!

The resurrection of the mustard seed culminates in a grand and joyous festival of birds.

All of history moves toward the Kingdom. From Christmas to Christmas. Always and only toward the Kingdom.

10

Jerusalem Prayers Go Round and Round

Luke 18:9–14

> *He also told this parable to some who trusted in themselves that they were righteous and regarded others with contempt: "Two men went up to the temple to pray, one a Pharisee and the other a tax collector. The Pharisee, standing by himself, was praying thus, 'God, I thank you that I am not like other people: thieves, rogues, adulterers, or even like this tax collector. I fast twice a week; I give a tenth of all my income.' But the tax collector, standing far off, would not even look up to heaven, but was beating his breast and saying, 'God, be merciful to me, a sinner!' I tell you, this man went down to his home justified rather than the other; for all who exalt themselves will be humbled, but all who humble themselves will be exalted."* NRSV

THIS EVENING Jesus takes us to the theatre to see *Jerusalem Prayers Go Round and Round*, an old-time drama where one sees two pious Jerusalemites engaged in prayer: an impeccable Pharisee on one side and a sinful tax collector on the other.

Let's look at the program. It's always important to consult the program, because that's where we find a summary of the play. This is indispensable so we won't be taken by surprise. The program says that he spoke to some people who prided themselves on being virtuous and despised everyone else. No surprise possible here; it's completely clear. We're going to have a good person (despised) and a bad person (despising). In the theatre of the Bible, the bad one is always the Pharisee, the one who prays with his head high, with one eye on God and one eye on his neighbor. One eye fluttering and tearful, like in the pious and theatrical prayers of time past (that is the eye on God), and one eye clear, quick and sharp, to accurately calculate, appreciate, and measure the difference between oneself and the "publicans," who are small in every way, especially when it comes to praying in the Temple.

To be a Pharisee is literally, in Aramaic, "to be separated." The ideal for the Pharisee is always to be separated, separable, to have a distinctive way of being, of living, of praying; consequently, to be "distinguished," detached from the others. The Pharisee is the bad guy who always maintains, whatever the cost, a separation from the others whom he "despises." That is what the program says.

It is a real theatre, with wings. And at a certain moment in the play Jesus takes us to visit the wings. An extraordinary privilege! Normally, we see only what is on stage. No one has the right to go backstage, to have this deeper view, to see the other side of the cards. Normally, we see only the scenery and the show, but how then can one come to understand the secret and hidden ways of the bad Pharisee? Only a detour into the wings reveals everything to us. And now we see the other side of the cards: the Pharisee prayed thus "to himself . . ." You can see what a privilege this is: we are capable not only of seeing behind, but also of *seeing inside* how the Pharisee prays "to himself."

This is the real play. Now we see all; even what was hidden, like God sees. We see the front side and the back side, the outside and the inside, the façade and everything that was going on "in himself." This evening we have witnessed the interior of a Pharisee in prayer!

Jesus left us at our leisure to do and to see, but just then things began to get complicated . . .

Did this Pharisee really show the negative signs of being a bad person? We began to look uneasily at ourselves. Is it a bad sign to fast twice a week? Is it a bad sign to give ten per cent of all we get? Is that bad piety, the bad interior of a man at prayer? So we hasten to take a look at the other prayer.

When we look again at the tax collector, things quickly appear to be a little overdone. Viewed from backstage, this "good" prayer appears less credible. He added on too much. He was an excellent actor, and very edifying. He acted marvelously. In any case, you couldn't miss him. He knew how to adopt the grand theatrical postures of former times. What talent! He beat his breast in sorrow. He groaned (but not to himself): he could be heard at the back of the room! What theatre! What a production!

Now the "good" and the "bad" are all mixed up. Wasn't it the supposed "good guy" who put on the best act? And we, who had read the summary before watching the play, and who knew how it ended ("he who humbles himself will be exalted and he who exalts himself will be humbled"), are perplexed. We ask ourselves: Wasn't it the latter, thoroughly "humbled," theatrically "humbled," who wins by taking the detour of humiliation to be better "exalted"?

And, to push our embarrassment even further, Jesus tells us: "this man went down to his house justified *and not the other.*" And this proposition does not settle the matter, for hasn't the pharisaic style of differences triumphed after all? For, to be justified *rather than the other*, is to have become a "Pharisee," a *separated one*, even if you still call yourself a publican. The difference from the other remains: I have become better than the other!

It seemed to us that the outcome of the play was that all was lost, *no one prayed*; neither the one who counted up all those good things that separated him from others; nor the one who held himself "apart," not by his perfections but by his show of spectacular imperfections! There were only Pharisees on stage, in relief or hidden, positive or negative, in good works or in great lamentations.

The next Sabbath, one could guess that everything would begin again but with the roles reversed. The ex-publican would say: "Thank you, Lord, for justifying me, me rather than the other;" and he could wear the Pharisee's costume from last week. And the ex-Pharisee this time would only have eyes for crying and groaning and perhaps (who knows?) he would beat his breast. And the following Sabbath, what would they do? Change roles again? Would it ever be possible one day to come to the Temple to pray? How could one ever be honestly humble if one knew that being humble was the best way to exalt oneself?

That was the play: the prayers go round and round in the Temple without ever managing to pray. Sometimes as a tax collector. Sometimes as a Pharisee. No matter which! No prayer is possible in that scheme, for "difference" from the others reigns. That is to say, finally, contempt: for oneself to be just, and not the others. *Without* the others.

As we leave the theatre, Jesus approaches us, his eyes full of his Gospel. Don't hesitate to leave this theatre of shadows behind! Why do you have such a short memory? This play of the two Prayers is only the shadow cast by the preceding story: the prayer of the widow for better justice in her city (Luke 18:1–8). That is where the true prayer is found, never given up.

To pray is not at all to seek one's own personal justice in a temple, but to battle to attain a good justice, certainly for oneself, but also for all the others, in the city. And to do this before going to the Temple!

Pharisaic friends and publican friends, the healing of our prayers will come always from the city. In truth, it can only come from there!

11

The True Vine

John 14:31—15:8
(Isaiah 5)

"Rise, let us be on our way.

"I am the true vine, and my Father is the vinegrower. He removes every branch in me that bears no fruit. Every branch that bears fruit he prunes to make it bear more fruit. You have already been cleansed by the word that I have spoken to you. Abide in me as I abide in you. Just as the branch cannot bear fruit by itself unless it abides in the vine, neither can you unless you abide in me. I am the vine, you are the branches. Those who abide in me and I in them bear much fruit, because apart from me you can do nothing. Whoever does not abide in me is thrown away like a branch and withers; such branches are gathered, thrown into the fire, and burned. If you abide in me, and my words abide in you, ask for whatever you wish, and it will be done for you. My Father is glorified by this, that you bear much fruit and become my disciples." NRSV

Here we have something more than a parable; it is also one of the most ancient hymns of Israel, a poem which for at least eight centuries has dwelt in Jerusalem and all the memories and hearts of Israel. It is a poem of a vine well loved and a vine abandoned. A poem of bitterness, for what have I not done for my vine? He hoped for some fruits, but nothing. It is a vine thrown to the wild beasts, trod under foot, ruined ... Listen, Israel! Nothing but unhappiness and violence ...

"Rise, let us be on our way" (14:31), says Jesus. And with that, everything begins. It is night, no doubt one of the last. They must seek refuge outside the city walls. The troubled little group follows Jesus. They leave the city and go down toward the Kidron Valley. It is night. The dry vine branches crack underfoot. It is the vine. And the little band enters the night, enters the vine. They enter the poem of the vine.

We must follow Jesus there. Not in what he says, for at the beginning he says nothing. He listens. It is night, and all noises become suspect, signals to decipher. They are like signs of disquieting presences, especially when you are hunted and afraid. Jesus listens to the night, and in the night the complaint of the vine dresser about the much loved vine is awakened in his memory.

All of this is in play: respect for the night that sings and Jesus' respectful listening to the vine that speaks to him.

The little nighttime band enters into this sorrowful song which always ends badly with destruction and death. It is a funeral song, a hymn of the destruction of the vine.

Let's get out of here! Already Judas has left us, denounced us, and plotted against us. Already Peter has warned us that he is a likely turncoat. Miserable team. It is truly night.

Suddenly the vine groans underfoot. Is it the end? He had hoped for some fruit, but there is nothing, nothing but disappointment. Jesus listens and recites to himself the ancient song. The eight-centuries-old vine speaks to him. Lost vine. Abandoned Son. Broken fence. Everyone hesitates, because each step makes the vine cry. And the other's step adds to the plaintive cracking sound that I have created. The slightest movement brings on weeping. The night is everywhere, and the poem also. It is the song of the death of the vine.

Jesus and his companions are troubled. Across the fields and the centuries a song of sorrow has reached them. And now they understand these last hours much better. Jesus thinks, and says to them: I am the vine. All is finished. All is lost.

On this night Jesus' troubled little band has become the final verse, living in flesh and blood Israel's ancient song. Together they have become a word, speech. Jesus crosses this vineyard as a garden of Gethsemane. Why, my God, do you abandon your vine? Must he really go all the way, become a vine trampled on, scorned, renounced, crucified? In the night everyone listens to the old wounded and healing plants. They walk on the dry branches. And Jesus is sad unto death. I am the vine . . . Is it already the last night?

Word. In this vineyard everything becomes word. And near to Kidron this is what they hear: "You have already been cleansed by the word that I have spoken to you." Already clean . . .

As the plant seeks and hopes for its fruit, the Word seeks and hopes for the mouth of the one who will bring it to the world, make it audible, present it among men and women. I am the Word and you are my mouths, carriers of my words and my fruits. I am the root buried in the soil, old wounded plant; you, be my voice, be vowels, cries of hope, living vines, fruits of the sun after my cross.

We must not make too big a distinction between the trunk and the branches. It is better simply to say "vine." For the vine is an ensemble, a whole life, a history, a heritage. The vine is the trunk, the branches both cut and shaped, an enclosure, and of course, a vinegrower, many of them, and this great and foolish hope that the vinegrower has for his vine. We must recover this ensemble, this fundamental solidarity, this necessity of all being there, in order to be "vine." The poem says it again and again: no trunk without branches, no branches without trunk. I in you. You in me. And no vine without the vinegrower. No vinegrower without the vine. We have here just a single drama, which goes from the vinegrower all the way to the cut branch. A single hope.

I am the vine, this unity. I in you. You in me. And the life of the vinegrower is in your hands. The Gospel of the vine is that together we are the promise of the harvest and of life. Or of a terrible night of despair.

I am the vine. I am walking toward the cross; but you, you are to be my fruit. My stock is living its final nights, but I want you to be the new growth of the morning of my resurrection. Together, remain a vine: chosen, loved, honed, murdered, shaped, wounded, but fecund!

Through night and vine, we descend toward Kidron. Afterword, it will suffice to come back up. The other side is the Garden of Olives, the end.

Now, those around Jesus know. I, Jesus, walk to the cross, but you are to be my voice, speak my words, bear my fruits.

Suddenly, the night is torn away to give way to the great clarity of Golgotha. "The branch lives only if it is attached to the vine." This cry from Kidron cuts across and through all the darkness and all the Good Fridays. Only those will live forever who remain attached to the root. The vine's complaint covers all. Only those will live who remain attached to the root.

Jesus and his companions go. All is accomplished. The vine has spoken. *Only those live who are hung from the wood.*

I walk toward the cross; but you, you are to be my fruits. I am going to die and remain attached to the wood. Please be the new growth, the shoots, of resurrection!

I am the vine. . . . But then what is the vinegrower doing?

12

The Gospel Begins at Cana

JOHN 2:1–11

On the third day there was a wedding in Cana of Galilee, and the mother of Jesus was there. Jesus and his disciples had also been invited to the wedding. When the wine gave out, the mother of Jesus said to him, "They have no wine." And Jesus said to her, "Woman, what concern is that to you and to me? My hour has not yet come." His mother said to the servants, "Do whatever he tells you." Now standing there were six stone water jars for the Jewish rites of purification, each holding twenty or thirty gallons. Jesus said to them, "Fill the jars with water." And they filled them up to the brim. He said to them, "Now draw some out, and take it to the chief steward." So they took it. When the steward tasted the water that had become wine, and did not know where it came from (though the servants who had drawn the water knew), the steward called the bridegroom and said to him, "Everyone serves the good wine first, and then the inferior wine after the guests have become drunk.

But you have kept the good wine until now." Jesus did this, the first of his signs, in Cana of Galilee, and revealed his glory; and his disciples believed in him. NRSV

THE MARRIAGE feast at Cana and the changing of a great quantity of water into very good wine marks the beginning of Jesus' ministry in the Gospel of John. A dazzling debut! In John's Gospel this narrative takes the place that the other synoptic gospels give to the Temptation of Jesus. Here, however, it is not a matter of the Temptation of Jesus strictly speaking, but rather of putting Jesus' first disciples to the test (they having been gathered in the immediately preceding verses).

Both the narrative of the Temptation of Jesus and that of testing the disciples belong to the same literary genre: the supernatural fantastic that is frequently found in ancient mythologies. To the compacted, but imaginary, discussion between a Satan and Jesus entering into his ministry corresponds, here, an overflowing, but imaginary, multiplication of wine. There, Satan said: out of these stones, make bread! Here, Jesus replies: from water, make wine! In both instances we are in the allegorical world of testing rituals to which all postulants must submit.

The disciples can be divided into three groups: the friends of John the Baptist, the reformer from the desert;[1] the orthodox and guileless Nathanael;[2] finally the judeo-greek group represented by Philip, who bears a Hellenic name.[3]

1. John 1:35–42.
2. John 1:47–51.
3. John 1:43–45.

These three types of disciples are about to undergo the test of the Wedding of Cana. And, let us note right off that the narrative concludes by saying that the disciples have successfully passed the test. We read in verse 11: "his disciples believed in him." Delivered, as we will soon see, from their false understandings of the Messiah, they are ready to enter "into the gospel."

I note also that the evangelist underscores that we have here "the first of Jesus' signs," the one which inaugurates his ministry and from which all the other signs will receive their form and meaning. Is it necessary to emphasize as well the boldness of this first sign? A wedding in Galilee lasted seven to eight days and involved the entire village. Jesus arrived late and joined a group that had already drunk quite a bit—so much that there was a shortage of wine. It is in this context that the Gospel begins, with what some will call a miracle of drunkenness! And to this Jesus does not hesitate to add 150 gallons of wine for guests who were already "tipsy" (v. 10)!

First test, first rectification. No to the moralists.

It is almost certain that John the Baptist and his disciples came from the religious milieu of the Essenes. Therefore, the shock and the appropriateness of the test, for the Essenes took vows of celibacy, continence, and asceticism. How upsetting for Essenes to be called to follow this new Master, this Unknown, whose first sign consists of celebrating what they considered improper for the Kingdom of God: a marriage!

Thus, the first rectification to make before following Jesus is to discover that the Gospel is not opposed to marriage and to the sexual union of man and woman. To the contrary, marriage is seen as a first sign of human joy. Far from putting it down, the Gospel celebrates conjugal happiness. With Jesus there is no place for the ascetics of the desert, the teetotalers, and the voluntary celibates. The Gospel is not of water, but of wine. It is not continence, but a festival of abundance.

150 more gallons of wine for the love of couples: that is Jesus. What a shock for water drinkers! "Everyone serves the good wine first, and then the inferior wine after the guests have become drunk."

That is the Gospel: till you are no longer thirsty.

One enters the gospel only after passing this test. Life is not mortification, but a festival. Every person originates in a festival!

Second rectification: for Nathanael, the guileless Jew. *No to the ritualists.*

Nathanael accepts everything that is sanctioned by religious ritual. So upon his arrival he was reassured to see, at the entrance to the house, the six stone jars for the purification rituals. His type of religious person believes that nature is not bad, but rather lacking, and that ritual is able to add a supernatural grace to nature in order to sanctify it. Marriage, for example, is legitimate if the proper ritual is performed.

Nathanael rejoices when he sees the six jars. It is acceptable to drink and make love because all that is blessed by ritual. Soon, the purification rite will transmute ugly lead into the beautiful gold of the Law and the Prophets. And, look, Jesus is about to fill all the jars!

It is then that Nathanael, learned and attentive Jew, discovers the revolution that is playing out: water is turning into wine. Water belongs to the system of filth which must be washed. Wine, on the contrary, is the most beautiful gift of God. It gladdens God's heart and makes it rejoice. That is the new gospel that Nathanael is called to believe and live: human life is an exalting adventure. And the marriage of this couple of Cana, for example, is like an image of the joys of the Kingdom. Man and woman, united by marriage, are truly, as the beautiful Creation poem says, an "image of God:" the gift of self for the joy and life of the other. Such a festival has no need of ritual to be just and beautiful!

Third test: for Philip. *No to the mystics.*

To get drunk, through religious practices of course, is to enter into a second condition where the demons and cares of everyday life are blurred and the limits of our earthly condition are overcome. Like every kind of "ecstasy," drunkenness lets us leave behind the conditions of our existence and escape from our bonds. We forget everything that is contingent and fly away to heaven. That is the exploit of the mystics. Philip loves that supplement afforded by drunkenness. 150 more gallons to regain paradise. It is the same story as with drugs: anticipate beginning now the end and fullness of history. Divine drunkenness, sacred drug, mystical piety—they all have the same goal: an immediate short-circuit between heaven and earth.

The mother of Jesus was also of this "type." It was she who called to Jesus and said, "They have no wine." She was right. It was true. She implored: they lack something (as the saying goes).

Philip had great hopes for this unexpected overdose.

It is in this way that a double breaking of time is produced. Jesus' mother discovers that it is too early: my hour has not yet come! And the steward observes that it is too late: they are already sotted, and now you serve the good wine! The suitable hour for this wine has passed!

All mystical drunkenness is always out of place. Between too early and too late there is no temporal space possible, no present time. There is only absence or missed rendezvous.

Philip and the mother of Jesus must take a different route if they want to follow Jesus. "Heaven" is not found far from others and beyond the present, but with others, in daily life and from below. The gospel says no to mystical escapes. On purpose Jesus arrived at the marriage at the wrong time and late.

It was at Cana. Beginning with the union of the two spouses that he celebrated as his first sign, Jesus raised a warning against moralism and asceticism, against obligatory rituals, and against the ridiculous illusions of the mystics.

It was at Cana, and *the disciples believed in him.*

13

Zechariah, the Mute Prophet

Luke 1:5–13, 18–23

In the days of King Herod of Judea, there was a priest named Zechariah, who belonged to the priestly order of Abijah. His wife was a descendant of Aaron, and her name was Elizabeth. Both of them were righteous before God, living blamelessly according to all the commandments and regulations of the Lord. But they had no children, because Elizabeth was barren, and both were getting on in years.

Once when he was serving as priest before God and his section was on duty, he was chosen by lot, according to the custom of the priesthood, to enter the sanctuary of the Lord and offer incense. Now at the time of the incense offering, the whole assembly of the people was praying outside. Then there appeared to him an angel of the Lord, standing on the right side of the altar of incense. When Zechariah saw him, he was terrified; and fear overwhelmed him. But the angel said to him, "Do not be afraid, Zechariah, for your prayer has been heard. Your wife Elizabeth will bear you a son, and you will name him John." . . . Zechariah said to the angel, "How will I know that this is so? For I am an old man, and my wife is getting on in years." The angel replied, "I am Gabriel. I stand in the presence of God, and I have been sent to speak to you and bring you this good news. But now, because you did not believe my words, which will be fulfilled in their time, you will become mute and unable to speak, until the day these things occur."

Meanwhile the people were waiting for Zechariah, and wondered at his delay in the sanctuary. When he did come out, he could not speak to them, and they realized that he had seen a vision in the sanctuary. He kept motioning to them and remained unable to speak. When his time of service was ended, he went to his home. NRSV

I LOVE Luke the Evangelist a lot. The Christmas Play that he has written and put on stage for his congregation in Rome is admirable. All of Rome has its place in it: the Emperor and the little shepherds, the old people and the newborn, men and women, celebrated actors and those in minor roles; yes, the world is there, even the angels! This way all of Rome is able to hear the Gospel of the Liberator.

We must begin with the first character to appear on stage: Zechariah. He doesn't say much, but all by himself he puts us on the path of hope.

Zechariah waits. He is defined by his waiting. He has asked for a son and, stubborn, he sits there, in his corner, waiting. He waits even beyond all common sense, but what does that matter! His wife is sterile and he is worn out, but he waits for a son, his son. It is *fifty years* that Zechariah has waited when the curtain rises.

Now Zechariah is more than Zechariah: he is a priest in the section of Abijah and therefore designated to burn incense in the temple. Since the Exile, this offering had taken on a great importance in Israel for it was the visible sign of the offering to God of the prayers of the people. Zechariah figures then in a waiting that is both personal and collective: a wait for a son who would be for all of Israel. This means, then, that in fact it has been *five hundred years* that Zechariah has waited for the curtain to rise.

Moreover, that is not to say enough. Who doesn't see that? This old family goes back to the beginning of Israel and brings to mind Abraham and Sarah. They are the original, first and founding, couple. A sterile couple who as such are father and mother of the son of miracle and hope. Zechariah-Elizabeth is the last possible way of saying Abraham-Sarah. The whole history of Israel is there. Zechariah-Elizabeth, a prayer worn out and ineffective. They are old, very old. So *two thousand years* of waiting when the curtain rises.

But to say only that is to leave us out of the Christmas Play. These are characters too large for us. Who has prayed two thousand years without weakening? Of whom among us can it be written: "Both of them were righteous before God, living blamelessly according to all the commandments and regulations of the Lord"? Will this festival have to take place without us?

Happily, Zechariah is only so great on the rebound. Truth to tell, he is also the one to whom it is said: "Because you did not believe my words . . . you will become mute and unable to speak." In that Zechariah I can recognize myself.

Had he truly asked for a son? Hardly. For why all of a sudden is he astonished and asks, How is it possible? Having entered into the very movement which leads to his prayer being answered, suddenly he is unmasked. After all, he had never really believed that it would be possible for him to have a son. Certainly, he had prayed; but look at his surprise. When I was mumbling my disappointment, was there someone listening to me? How could that be? . . . He hadn't truly prayed, but nonetheless he had truly been heard. I mumbled like that in the solitude of an old man. I told myself about it, but no one else. . . . Who then listened to me?

This is the Zechariah who speaks to me, who touches me. He is the man that I am. He has never prayed, and at Christmas he discovers that he has nonetheless always prayed! The answer to his prayer reveals to him the emptiness of his former pious blabbing. But, by grace and in hindsight, in spite of himself, this answer reconstitutes for him a true prayer. Two thousand years of little bits of prayer, little bits of waiting. Fifty years of pious egoistic chit-chat. Nothing. Sterile. Impotence. Of non-prayer. An entire history slightly flawed, with gestures and habits that one doesn't want to abandon but which one secretly doubts. And that's what Christmas is: all of a sudden someone who takes you at your word.

Yes, *to be taken at one's word*, that is the festival! To go from mere talk to confronting a promise which is realized. I, too, I said it like that: the Son, the Son, without really believing it. And now he is there! And now Zechariah must go there. And you must go, to this Son. . . . Zechariah goes, but demands a sign; he wants to be a prophet.

We mustn't be mistaken about this demand for a sign. In our modern culture that would represent a mark of unbelief. But in the Bible it is completely otherwise. When one asks for a sign, it is that one knows that everything is already decided and in place and that one wants to make it appear that one has decided it oneself. In order not to lose face too much. Asking for a sign is a sort of polite deal between each prophet and his Lord. That is why Zechariah will demand and receive the sign which will make him a real prophet.

A strange prophet of the New Covenant, for it is by becoming mute that he will be eloquent! It is by losing his voice that he will come to speech! "When he did come out, he could not speak to them, and they realized."

Paradoxical prophet, maker of signs: he made signs to them and remained unable to speak.

How we are like Zechariah since Christmas! All has begun. The son has already begun to be formed in the womb of Elizabeth, just as the Kingdom is already in process of being built in the womb of an apparently sterile history. In a sense, we have been given the message, but it is impossible for us to speak of it otherwise than by the detour and enigma of signs.

From then on that will always be true for the prophets of the New Covenant. They speak without speaking for others, without speaking in their place. They speak without saying. They push others in a difficult interpretation. That is the grandeur (and not the misery) of the Word of which one can never say enough. Whoever hears it must him or herself set about to speak.

Zechariah is an exemplary prophet: he makes others speak. A whole crowd. For the Gospel of Luke, that's what Christmas is: the Word has come to live with us. The Word speaks because it makes us speak, all of us, of the Liberator of the world.

Zechariah mute. Elizabeth sterile. But both of them bent by the hope that works through their history and that of the world.

My friend, your little hope and your waiting and your tired prayers, all of that has with one stroke been taken seriously by the Lord himself. It is true. The Kingdom is underway. From now on it is up to you to be a sign and mute word of the Lord.

14

A Healing of Communication

Luke 7:1–10

After Jesus had finished all his saying in the hearing of the people, he entered Capernaum. A centurion there had a slave whom he valued highly, and who was ill and close to death. When he heard about Jesus, he sent some Jewish elders to him, asking him to come and heal his slave. When they came to Jesus, they appealed to him earnestly, saying, "He is worthy of having you do this for him, for he loves our people, and it is he who built our synagogue for us." And Jesus went with them, but when he was not far from the house, the centurion sent friends to say to him, "Lord, do not trouble yourself, for I am not worthy to have you come under my roof; therefore I did not presume to come to you. But only speak the word, and let my servant be healed. For I am also a man set under authority, with soldiers under me; and I say to one, 'Go,' and he goes, and to another, 'Come,' and he comes, and to my slave, 'Do this,' and he does it." When Jesus heard this he was amazed at him, and turning to the crowd that followed him, he said, "I tell you, not even in Israel have I found such faith." When those who had been sent returned to the house, they found the slave in good health. NRSV

With Jesus' healings there is always more healing than expected. Above all, when Luke tells the story. It is as if the healthy energy brought by Jesus was capable of modifying not only the sick but also those around by a sort of contagion of renewed life.

Very often, and in every sense of the word, the sickness is taken to be a *sickness of communication* that prevents people from communicating with one another, a sickness that expels someone out of the social group, that isolates and closes people off from one another. It is not for nothing that the sick in the gospels are blind, deaf, mute, paralyzed, leprous, etc., that is, those who can no longer normally enter into relations with others. They cannot see them, hear them, speak with them, walk with them, live among them, etc.

All of this is true of the narrative of the servant of the Roman centurion of Capernaum. And the healing of communication that Jesus accomplishes constitutes the most beautiful possible Gospel for all sick people.

There are three observations to develop.

First observation, on the setting.
The text indicates that it is very difficult to establish communication between Jesus and the centurion who must speak with him without seeing or meeting him.

We must emphasize this strange setting that is unique to Luke. In Matthew's parallel telling, everything takes place much more simply, more directly, through a moving face to face encounter between a supplicant centurion and a Lord passing through the city. Luke has completely dropped the face to face meeting. In his story, Jesus *will never see* either the slave or the centurion who remains in his house. Contact is established indirectly by two different sets of ambassadors. First, it is "some Jewish elders" (some leaders from the synagogue), then soldiers from the centurion's company coming to plead for a beneficent intervention by Jesus. It is exclusively through these two groups that the centurion seeks to speak to Jesus.

At the end, when the bedridden servant is healed the difficult circuit of speaking is also healed. It makes one think that for Luke the healing of spoken communication is a parable of the physical healing of the sick servant.

Second observation, on the tactics of healing.

Healing can begin only when one agrees to upset the established order, even if that order has been in place for ever. An upset order is a sign that healing is coming.

I want to accent several reversals of established order in the actions described by Luke. Several times hierarchies are reversed. Nearly every time there is a new and surprising redistribution of roles.

Let's look.

It happens with the centurion. At that time it would be unheard of for the captain of a Roman garrison to be concerned about the health of one of his boys, probably a Jewish one, and to take steps to heal him. This is a first shift in relations that announce something new. An officer is at the service of a servant!

Something similar happens with the important Jews called "elders." If they in fact are leaders of the local synagogue, they are also violently opposed to Rome (and to its occupying armies) and to Jesus, considered to be a friend of sinners and thus as a disturber of the established religion. Yet, although opposed to Rome and Jesus, this group will bring about their connection by agreeing (this tops everything) to plead the cause of a Roman before a questionable pseudo-Messiah. This is both fundamental and unimaginable. It is much more than challenging habits and hierarchical organization. It overturns profound and ancestral convictions.

But we also find a great change for Jesus. Usually, he is the one who speaks, and others are delighted to listen to him. Usually, he tells parables that astonish and intrigue. But here it is Jesus who listens to a little pagan parable: when I, the captain, give orders, I am obeyed without hesitation. Luke presents Jesus as a happy and amazed auditor of this little Roman military story. A third rupture is that he who is regarded as the Word of God discovers that this may mean being an attentive listener to a pagan. Everything shifts. The most solid foundations crack. Everything is mixed up. Characters leave their prescribed role and begin to live another life. Everyone agrees to go toward the other. It is this unfreezing of acquired positions that prepares and announces the healing of the servant, and much more than the servant!

Third observation: provoked by the urgency of a call for help, communication begins thanks to intermediaries and proceeds in spite of them.

This is the heart of the story of healing. The intermediaries are both necessary and insignificant. Yes, they transmit, but by betraying.

Since Jesus and the centurion will never see one another in the story, it is clear that nothing can begin without the mediation of the two intermediaries, the two ambassadors sent by the centurion to Jesus.

How does that unroll on the road? In truth, not very well.

The first ambassadors, the Jewish elders, come and plead "as Jews." How could they have done otherwise?

They are a virtual caricature of religion. They deliver the centurion's request in their own religious language, rather disagreeable, in which the calculation of religious and national merits take priority. "He is worthy of having you do this for him, for he loves our people, and it is he who built our synagogue for us." He is worthy because he thinks like us and has given us a very large gift . . .

It is just like that that one speaks in religious circles, especially in the religion of works. Consequently, alas, the plea of a tearful centurion becomes a sort of market (contract) where one measures what one will give in exchange for what one has received. Given giving. He is worthy of "so much."

This is the first transmission, translation, and betrayal. For it is not a simple matter to communicate, that is, to get out of oneself, just as it is not simple to heal. From whence, then, will come help?

Second ambassadors: the soldiers.

Since it is necessary, whatever the cost, to get a message from the centurion to Jesus, this second attempt is welcome.

This time soldiers close to the centurion bring his request to Jesus. Of course, they speak as they can, as they are, that is, as military men! And they present almost a caricature of life in the barracks. There you hear orders. Go!, and you go. Come!, and you come. Stand up! Forward march! It is condensed language. Words are reduced to being only commands. They bang and function like blows of a hammer. But it is true that that is how one communicates in the army. And the plea of the tearful centurion takes on the strange tone of exercises in the courtyard of the barracks. Forward march! Here! Bedridden! Healed!

Thus, the second transmission-translation-betrayal. Nevertheless, in spite of these bad relays, something like speech is passed, and it is this laborious birth of speech that gains Jesus' "admiration."

Perhaps there are no good relays, nor good pleas, nor good witnesses. Perhaps they are all false and botched. But perhaps we must (and in full knowledge) accept that imperfect relays are nevertheless relays! The important thing is to be what one is, and as such to put oneself at the service of the slave who needs healing.

Everyone has listened. Everyone has conveyed. Certainly, everyone has betrayed, but Jesus admires. They have all given themselves over to a suffering to be assuaged and a slave to free.

Consequently, healing begins. The Jews remain Jews; the soldiers remain Romans; and Jesus is neither Pharisee nor soldier!

But among all of them communication happens anyway.

The cradle of the speech that works is the emergency help to be brought to the little ones. That speech can heal; it can become alive among strangers and in several languages.

I have one concluding question. Where is the greatest miracle in this story of healing?

One could say (and this is manifestly evident), the most marvelous is the slave made healthy and restored to life. What could be more true? But Luke's telling does not highlight this marvel. The healing is done off-stage, without anyone on stage knowing of it. Even Jesus never speaks of it!

One could say the greatest miracle is the faith of the centurion. According to Luke, that would be Jesus' point of view. But I suspect (and may I be pardoned for this!) that that is rather the evangelist's point of view, he being happy to support the opinion of the Apostle Paul that pagans are more accessible to the Gospel than the best of the Jews of Israel.

One could also say that the most marvelous is the extraordinary courage of these Jews who have agreed to set aside their political and theological a prioris, or the boldness of these soldiers who dared to bestow on Jesus (even without knowing its full importance) the title that they should reserve for the emperor: "Lord."

Or perhaps the miracle is located on the side of Jesus who has, for once, witnessed a miracle, the birth of real speech, and who has been taught by an anonymous pagan military officer, and who thus has discovered that one always needs a stranger to heal his speech.

In fact, the miracle bursts forth here and everywhere. Healing has touched everyone! It dwells in (and therefore works in) each one's body, heart, language, and spirit.

Here is what is marvelous about this miracle: the difficult and necessary solidarity among Jews, Romans, Jesus, pagans, professionals from religion and the military. And why did this happen? So that a slave could be happy!

15

The Widow's Last Penny

MARK 12:41–44

He sat down opposite the treasury, and watched the crowd putting money into the treasury. Many rich people put in large sums. A poor widow came and put in two small copper coins, which are worth a penny. Then he called his disciples and said to them, "Truly I tell you, this poor widow has put in more than all those who are contributing to the treasury. For all of them have contributed out of their abundance; but she out of her poverty has put in everything she had, all she had to live on." NRSV

THE FIRST thing that surprises me is that Matthew, alone, has refused to reproduce this brief episode that he read in Mark's Gospel. Jesus observes many people presenting their offerings in the Temple. After seeing a widow give her last penny, he declared, "all of them have contributed out of their abundance; but she out of her poverty has put in everything she had, all she had to live on." ["live" from *bios,* "life"] What was so scandalous to Matthew's church that he cut out this episode pure and simple?

We should note that Matthew usually follows Mark faithfully. Mark is his source, to which he adds new information. Of the 103 pericopes in the Gospel of Mark, Matthew leaves out only 9! In general the reasons for these decisions are understandable. For example, when Mark tells how demons confess the divinity of Jesus[1] (It would indeed be incongruous to have a parallel between what Matthew's church regularly confesses and the diabolical cry of demons!) or when Mark notes that Jesus' family worried that he had lost his senses and tried to stop him![2] But in this case it is difficult to grasp right away the reasons for a total censure. What is there here that scandalizes Matthew?

A widow has come *to complete her life* in the Temple. She has come to give her whole life, her entire *bios.* What does Jesus see and observe in this dramatic act? What word does he understand? It is clear that this widow speaks to him of death, but whose death, the death of what?

It would be too little to say that this is to be understood as the gospel of the death of the Temple and of its religion. Moreover, that question will be openly raised in the very next passage: "Not one stone here will be left upon another; all will be thrown down." Matthew never hid that Jesus led a decisive and permanent battle against the Temple, the sacrifice, and the priests of Jerusalem. Each healing not sanctioned by a sacrifice in the Temple was an

1. Mark 1:23–28; 1:34; 3:11.
2. Mark 3:20–21.

open and almost daily attack against that religion. It was the same for each Sabbath and day of fasting not observed. And remember his magisterial attempt to cleanse the Temple with the gospel of "the whip of cords." (No more holy money, no more purchase of animals, and even no more animals to sell because sacrifices are no more; that is, a dead Temple!) One of Jesus' first parables of the Kingdom was clearly challenging to religion: the New Covenant is nothing more than a little *leaven* added to the dough.[3] So with one stroke all the mountains of ancient sacrifices are annulled, those whose sole greatness was precisely to be "without leaven." Matthew never hesitated to celebrate the gospel of a little bit of leaven. And with leaven nothing of the religion of the Old Covenant remains. *Nothing.* So it is not the death of the Temple that is announced in Mark. It is not that which led Matthew to censor Mark's Gospel. There must be something more scandalous, not only for the Jews, but finally for Matthew's parishioners in Jesus' words: "For all of them have contributed out of their abundance; but she out of her poverty has put in everything she had, all she had to live on."

Jesus watched. What did the widow say to him with her unnerving end of life?

This widow commits here a very strange act, an act of solitude, the act of a widow, nearly secret, as anonymous as the woman herself. If no one had observed it, it would have had no eloquence, no impact on another. It would have been an act without consequences. For sure, Jesus will provide consequences for this solitary act. He will speak of it

3. Matthew 13:33.

to his disciples and establish a parallel with the rich givers. But, precisely, it is he who will create a parallel. The widow put herself on a parallel trajectory without any hope of an encounter, a crossing, an intersection, or of relation with the trajectories of others.

We have here an act out of the norm, asocial, in tangent to all of history, an escape toward infinity. It is an act of tranquil violence, absolutely deadly, a sort of silent murder against herself. We are projected beyond all morality, all religion. "She has drawn from her poverty and has thrown in her sustenance, her entire life."

At the dawn of the Old Covenant there also was a founding act, a gesture of extreme and insupportable violence. It was Abraham raising the knife against his son. Will the New Covenant open with another insupportable founding act?

Abraham and his son went out early in the morning with several servants. When they had come near to the altar at Moriah, Abraham went ahead alone with his son. The two of them were alone for an act without witnesses, secret, silent, an act of impressive solitude. They had prepared everything, brought everything, except for what was "necessary" (the victim). They had more than enough of what was "superfluous." They moved toward a sacrifice where *in order to protect the necessary, they separated it from the superfluous*. And in the thicket a superfluous ram was caught by the horns in the bushes. Substitution. To give "lots of the superfluous" to protect the necessary.

In the *Old Covenant* Abraham's act was stopped, *in extremis*. It was the time of religion and of sacrifices, and the terrible act of Abraham was transformed into an animal sacrifice. This was a founding act of Jewish sacrifices.

In the *New Covenant* the widow's act will not be stopped. For we are no longer in the realm of religion and sacrifices, even in the Jerusalem Temple. This time, Jesus is watching. He sees there silent death, disappearance. It is the end of sacrifices, and perhaps much more than that! End of the Old Covenant! End of the God of sacrifices!

The Old Testament has always given much, much out of its extra. The hour has come to give from its lack, its non-having, its non-being, that is, all of its *bios* . . .

Mark thinks, it seems, that *Jesus dies like the widow*. That is why he places this encounter at a decisive moment, just before Passover and the Feast of Unleavened Bread. Before his end arrived, Jesus, watching the widow, saw himself walking toward death. Like the widow, Jesus will die because he will have drawn beyond his lack. It is not because he was rich, but because he was nothing, emptied, the absolute Poor One.

Matthew, and especially his Judeo-Christian congregation, could not go that far. They would search in the bushes to find a lamb for the sacrifice. For they wanted to save what they saw as a sacrifice, namely, the Cross. For them, the widow's act will be only a repeat of Abraham's act, where everything ends in sacrifice.

There is *total opposition* between the two readings. Either Jesus on the Cross is offered as a sacrifice or Jesus dies like the widow, having no sacrifice to offer because he has already given everything. His is the death of one who is absolutely poor.

If God is no longer a god of sacrifices, how are we now to speak of God?

For the Gospel, *God is the one who gives.* God receives nothing and takes nothing, God gives all that God has, all that God is. God is love without condition and without return. God is grace. Nothing but grace.

16

The Shepherd

JOHN 10:1–6, 22

"Very truly, I tell you, anyone who does not enter the sheepfold by the gate but climbs in by another way is a thief and a bandit. The one who enters by the gate is the shepherd of the sheep. The gatekeeper opens the gate for him, and the sheep hear his voice. He calls his own sheep by name and leads them out. When he has brought out all his own, he goes ahead of them, and the sheep follow him because they know his voice. They will not follow a stranger, but they will run from him because they do not know the voice of strangers." Jesus used this figure of speech with them, but they did not understand what he was saying to them. . . . At that time the festival of the Dedication took place in Jerusalem. NRSV

THE ECLIPSE *of the Shepherd.*
I want to begin with a remark about the Scriptures' use of the image of the Shepherd.

Since David was reinterpreted as a shepherd, the Old Testament expectation of the Messiah readily used the figure of the Shepherd. The Shepherd functioned as a signal announcing the Messiah.

After Jesus, toward the end of the first century, the same thing that occurred in Israel took place in the Church. First was the Fourth Gospel (Parable of the Good Shepherd and Peter's function as Shepherd after Easter) followed by many texts in the Church Fathers. Once again, the symbol of the Shepherd dominated, from the *Didache* to the drawings on the walls of the catacombs: the Christ is the Shepherd.

Yet, this symbol, which was so clear and strong for the Old Testament and the second century, underwent a total eclipse during the period of Jesus' ministry. Neither Paul nor Mark, the earliest writers, made use of this eloquent image. After 80 C.E., in the celebrated Parable of the Lost Sheep, Matthew and Luke managed not to use the word "shepherd" even though it would have come naturally to them. Strangely, they repress this well-known symbol by writing, "Which of you, if you had one hundred sheep…?" This is a surprising eclipse of the most celebrated title in all of Scripture.

It seems to me that the most likely reason for this silence at the time of Jesus is that "shepherd" was a title appropriated by the Zealot movements. These messianic and revolutionary groups, who were the spiritual heirs of the unfortunate heroes of the Maccabean nationalist insurrection, formed small resistance bands that refused to pay taxes to Caesar and from time to time launched short-lived but deadly uprisings.

So it is understandable that in Jesus' time the title "shepherd" stood out so much that it had become suspect. One would hesitate to adopt a term claimed by terrorists. This would explain the silence up until 70 C.E., the date of the bitter failure of the violent nationalist movements.

This hypothesis is clearly supported by the Fourth Gospel. The Gospel is organized around "festivals." They give emphasis and mark like road signs the itinerary of Jesus' ministry. Moreover, the sequence of the Shepherd and his sheep pivots around a significant and clarifying affirmation for the whole: "At that time the festival of the Dedication took place in Jerusalem." This celebration commemorated the victory of the revolutionaries led by the Maccabees over Antiochus IV in 165 B.C.E. In the festive and overexcited context where the violence and shed blood of the ancestors was glorified the author was to write a parable of a pacific counter-shepherd. Or, rather, in this feverish and hysterical ambience, he wanted to demonstrate the corrective aim of the Gospel: Jesus has restored the proper meaning of the symbol of the Shepherd by distancing it from violent projects. The true Shepherd is Jesus and not one of the Maccabees.

Moreover, the author's choice of words is significant. The official term for the zealots was not "terrorists" (a modern designation) but "bandits" (Flavius Josephus). That term is used, for example, in the Parable of the Good Samaritan and for Barrabas as well as the two others crucified at the same time as Jesus. Thus, this official Roman terminology appears in the Parable of the Good Shepherd: that man is "a thief and a bandit." To the terrorist shepherd of the zealots, the Parable opposes the Shepherd of the Scriptures incarnated by Jesus.

The historical review is important because it reminds us of one of the several meanings of the title Shepherd. It is an image that easily tips toward the revolutionary side because it carries political connotations and evokes liberation of people. If one is not careful, this symbol quickly turns red!

When we speak on our own of the shepherd of the Parable, we make him gentle and sweet, charming among the bleating lambs, in pastel colors. But when we let the Parable speak for itself, the first thing that it says is this: Pastor (or Shepherd, the same thing) is a *very difficult title to wear*. The Pastor must not take to the hills, slide into violence, or allow himself to take up arms, but the Pastor must be so close to those things and to revolutionary hopes that, although wrong, people can have their suspicions of him.

A strange Shepherd, one who lives as close as possible to the revolution, who could pass for a liberation activist, but who refuses to fall into violence and terrorism. A strange Shepherd who is a sort of poet of revolution, prophet of subversion.

Such is the Good Shepherd in Jesus' time and in the circles where our Scriptures arose.

Outside! . . .
"He calls his own sheep by name and leads them *out . . .*"

This throws us off. When we speak on our own about the Parable we give the Shepherd a completely different function. Our shepherd gathers the flock, reunites it, is an agent of unity. We want the Pastor to serve the unity of the flock! But in the Parable the Shepherd is an agent of rupture. The Pastor calls the sheep in order to push them outside!

And it is not a matter of a little healthy walk to give the lambs some fresh air. It is much more serious. Jesus is announcing a terrible decision that he has just made, one which will lead to a sorrowful crisis. The moment has now come for him and his own to go outside Israel, that is, the Jewish theocracy, those around the synagogues who are the little bourgeois religious people of Jerusalem. A serious crisis is looming. He calls to his own and pushes them out of Israel!

According to the Fourth Gospel this has been provoked by the healing of a man born blind. The religious authorities have excommunicated the healed man because he was made free, physically and culturally, outside the forms and methods prescribed by the Law. Excommunicating a totally free man is the signal of rupture for Jesus. That is his revolution, his liberation of a people. He will lead his people outside of Israel, outside any religious institution. I am the Good Shepherd. I am giving birth to a new people outside the old ways. The old structure is irreparable, irreformable. We must leave all of that behind and depart. Outside!

He expels.

"When he has brought out [ἐκβάλη] all his own, he goes ahead of them."

The evangelist chooses an energetic and violent term: expel! The Shepherd acts with full determination and force to push outside the sheep that hesitate and hold onto the old chapel and fold. This is hard and painful work. It is like the suffering of a woman in labor who must make her baby "come out." To come out, that is life. To remain in the warm womb of Israel, that is death.

To live is to be placed in the world, put out there by the force of the Gospel.

When we speak on our own about the Parable, why do we give it such a different meaning? We say that the Pastor must at all cost keep the sheep warm and sheltered in the little stable where there are no problems! But when the Parable speaks for itself it says just the opposite. The lives of the sheep begin only when they go out, forced, toward the world. And the Shepherd is there to push them and walk ahead of them, leading them in an exodus toward life, in the "worldly" adventure of liberation.

The enemy of the sheep is not the outside but the "inside" when they remain there! The Shepherd will always work to shove us out of our securities of all kinds, to push us on the way to others, toward the gospel of freedom.

Today?

After all, around 90 to 100 C.E. it was rather easy to reread such a parable. The rupture between Christians and the Synagogue was accomplished and practically all the "departures" had taken place. It sufficed to encourage the last laggards. But what does it mean for us today? *Is this exodus still necessary*? Must it still be proclaimed? Or is the Parable extinct like an ancient star that has burned out all its fire?

For myself, I believe that the Parable still lives. I prefer to say that it still speaks. Its exhortation remains current.

The true Shepherd must still and always make his sheep go out toward the world, "place them in the world."

I believe in this paradox: the Church is both calling and departing, convocation and exodus. Doesn't that capture the full meaning of the Parable? The Shepherd calls (vocation and convocation) and he pushes outside (exodus and mission). The double movement is necessary. Without the call, how would we receive our "name" and our Christian identity? Without expulsion, we would abort and the Shepherd would make only still births!

To conclude, one more word, a terrible one, which shows precisely why the Parable will never "end," and why it must tomorrow and always be taken up again. We must keep this word in mind. Jesus told them this parable, but they understood nothing of what he had said to them. *Nothing!*

Jesus, strange and sorrowful Shepherd . . .

17

Sower, Nothing but the Sower

Mark 4:3–9

"Listen! A sower went out to sow. And as he sowed, some seed fell on the path, and the birds came and ate it up. Other seed fell on rocky ground, where it did not have much soil, and it sprang up quickly, since it had no depth of soil. And when the sun rose, it was scorched; and since it had no root, it withered away. Other seed fell among thorns, and the thorns grew up and choked it, and it yielded no grain. Other seed fell into good soil and brought forth grain, growing up and increasing and yielding thirty and sixty and a hundredfold." And he said, "Let anyone with ears to hear, listen!" NRSV

"MY THOUGHTS are not your thoughts, and your ways are not my ways, neither are your ways my ways. . . . For as the heavens are higher than the earth, so are my ways higher than your ways," said the Lord of Second Isaiah. Consequently, if a parable seeks to translate for us some of those thoughts so "higher than the earth," it is not surprising that we sometimes will have some difficulty understanding them well. This is also why parables, contrary to what one could think, carry with them many misunderstandings.

It is also why when Jesus spoke in parables his hearers wanted to hear (and therefore didn't understand) only allegories.

The parable is always disturbing, whereas the allegory reassures.

Yes, Jesus spoke in parables, but people wanted only to hear allegories. *Jesus spoke as a poet, but people only heard a teacher.* A teacher is one who speaks in our place, replaces us, and takes our place in the Word. He speaks and it suffices for us (as respondents) to say: Amen! The poet refuses to take the place of the other, doesn't want to speak in place of the other, for the other, in the name of the other. On the contrary, he wants to lead the other toward the creative risk of speaking a personal word. The poet makes the other speak.

In the allegory the teacher explains to us all the details: the rocky places are so and so, the thorny places are such and such, and the birds are Satan and his angels! . . . And so the Parable of the Sower becomes an allegory of soils, something that comforts us because, with it, we have the impression that we hold in our hands, possess, morsels of truth, no doubt in pieces, but that we can, like a puzzle, put the pieces together. Thus we fall back into our old traditional moralism: only the good soil, the good subjects, the good people, have a right to rewards, to good grades of B+, A, or even A+.

Jesus speaks in parables. He doesn't want to give us knowledge. His speech is not first of all a content, but a creation, and it is me who will be created a speaking person, a speaker. He makes us give birth to the Word. He makes us poets of our song, not repeaters of true sayings. I must become creator of a speech which is mine, his, and new.

Because of that Jesus' speech, that is, the parable, disturbs. It is like a surprising and unpredictable meteor of the Kingdom coming to upset and transgress our everyday soil and our human logic, by creating us as citizens of the Kingdom.

We must not let ourselves drift toward an allegory of soils (as the evangelists do), but do everything to read only the Parable of the Sower. Nothing else.

About this Parable Goethe once noted ironically that everywhere—absolutely everywhere, even the path!—was covered with seeds; even among thorns and in rocky places. A strange and admirable sower. He doesn't miss any kind of terrain. A crazy sower. Does he know what he is doing? Goethe spoke of a wasteful God! Personally, I like better a God who wastes his love than a penny-pinching God who would stingily measure out his mercy and grace. But in any case Goethe goes too far. Why speak of a wasteful God? Where is it a question of God? Let us stay with the Parable. Jesus speaks only of a sower. It is an opening parable, placed before several others. Here Jesus is presenting himself to Israel, to the crowds. Jesus says this is what I am: a sower! Nothing but a sower.

Let us tarry a moment over this original manner of presenting himself, this function that he chooses for representing himself: *a sower*.

My Jesus is not an agricultural machine destined to sow grain mechanically. He is a man of his time, not a superman, not an exceptionally gifted specialist. No. He is a man of his time, and he says: I have come out to sow, for I am a sower.

Machines make their rounds, almost by themselves. Jesus is a man who works. Moreover, he has more confidence in his seed than in himself. But he applies himself. I know: he is anxious, always wanting everything to be perfect, returning to "observe," and, if it is necessary, to do some more, to assure himself of the good quality of his work.

He doesn't want to be the cause, through negligence on his part, of his crop withering. Over there, for example, to be a bit more at ease, wouldn't it be good to add a little seed, to better cover the border, the corners, and the far ends? I hope, he says, that I have not forgotten a few bits of territory...

But, to sow takes only a few days. It is afterward that things really begin. Did I or did I not sow the seed? For a long time nothing comes out of the ground; there is no sign of growth. No one knows whether silently the seed is at work.

This waiting, that also is the sower. Besides, there is the fear of the possibility of drought, tornados or freezing. The sower will be anxious a long time without knowing.

Not, though, because of the seed, but because he is only the sower, not a machine, not a God.

And haven't you heard talk of the enemy of the sower, the one who comes in the night to sow weeds? The enemy of the night.

Yes, a sower is all of that: one full of hope and full of fear, one confident in his seed but always haunted by his nighttime enemy, the bringer of weeds.

It takes a long time for the fact of sowing to make of one a sower. Only at the end (note well what that means!), only at the end will he discover whether in fact he has been a sower.

"I have come out to sow." With that, in Israel, the scandal begins! It is a parable of opening, a parable-program. But right off Jesus disqualifies himself by speaking of sowing. Israel, by its culture, faith, and religion, waited for a Messiah who harvests, not a sower, a Son of Man who would come to conclude and crown a history, not to begin a new era. All the imagined Messiahs would announce themselves as the ones coming to finish, end, or complete time, in short, to harvest and not to inaugurate something new, to sow.

That is why people waited for a Messiah of glory and not of suffering, according to the proverb of the Psalmist of the Exile: "For the sowers, tears; but songs for the harvest." Or again: "The sower goes forth weeping. The harvester brings his sheaves home with shouts of joy!"[1]

Besides, the sowers were often absent at the time of the harvest festival. For the workers, pain and fatigue; for the

1. Psalm 126:5–6.

Master, the final glory and the full barns. "You know that I was a severe man . . . reaping what I did not sow," said the Master of the Parable of the Talents. "One sows and another reaps."[2] For the sower walks toward the death of the seed and the harvester returns from his resurrection!

This affirmation of sowing discredited Jesus. What a strange Messiah who wishes only to begin in tears, whereas everyone waited to see a Kingdom of glory burst forth!

I am a sower, nothing but a sower. I do not come to end anything, only to begin. I do not come as a flamboyant summer. I am a worker of cold earth at the end of winter.

Israel is baffled. But is it only Israel that is confused? Don't we still dream of another Jesus, a Jesus of the "end," Sovereign and Judge . . . and above all a Jesus who would open his granaries for us?

Jesus sower, *nothing but a sower.* Jesus without harvest, and dying too soon to rejoice over the ripe grain.

Humble Jesus of beginnings, my Lord.

---

2. Luke 19:22; John 4:37.

18

No More Cursed Fig Trees!

Luke 13:6–9

Then he told this parable: "A man had a fig tree planted in his vineyard; and he came looking for fruit on it and found none. So he said to the gardener, 'See here! For three years I have come looking for fruit on this fig tree, and still I find none. Cut it down! Why should it be wasting the soil?' He replied, 'Sir, let it alone for one more year until I dig around it and put manure on it. If it bears fruit next year, well and good; but if not, you can cut it down.'" NRSV

WHEN A fig tree without figs is mentioned, the one on the road from Bethany always comes to mind. After his entry into the capital, Jesus decided to spend the night with his friends Martha and Mary. While returning to Jerusalem the next day he is hungry and looks for figs on the roadside trees. He finds none, because it is not the season for figs. He is overcome with a fierce anger and curses the tree. Why? This cursing is really hard to understand! Why curse a tree for not producing fruit out of season, that is, if I may say so, accuse it for being a normal fig tree? "May no one ever eat fruit from you again." Very strange anger on Jesus' part . . .

I love it that Luke had the courage not to reproduce this wretched episode. By himself, he did all he could to erase it from our memory. He, and he alone, has written what we could call a counter story, a sort of anti-text of the Cursed Fig. He has given us the little remembered Parable of the Sterile Fig. Or, rather, a Parable of the Magnificent Gardener who dared, contrary to all expectation, to plead the cause of a tree that—just like the other one—hasn't produced figs.

We should remember this reversal in Luke's Gospel. I love this about face. It is in Luke's courage, more than anywhere else, that I hear the Gospel of Jesus of Nazareth.

So, here is Luke's Gospel (*the* Gospel): his Jesus does not kill trees. He takes their side and pleads for them, even if they do not bear fruit. He does this, even though many at that time would prefer to side with the Masters. Luke is in the other camp. His Jesus lines up with the trees, even unproductive ones, and thus against the Masters.

Yes, this is the Gospel of Jesus: we also must change sides; if necessary, change our Master, change our God!

The God of the Masters: No. The God of Jesus and his prejudice for the trees, even the dried up ones: Yes.

We must enter slowly into this Parable. It is already three years that the Master has come to pick fruit from his fig tree, planted in his vineyard, and he finds nothing. The gardener is called and receives the Master's order: cut it down!

It is clear that Luke has made of this Parable a caricature and a pamphlet. The Master is presented as a little oriental despot, a cruel and all-powerful god. He has the right of life and death over his subject and over all things. He says: "Cut it down!" and the tree dies. He could say: "May no one ever eat fruit from you again" and the tree would dry up immediately. With wild and impertinent audacity Luke suggests that there could be an analogy between this little barbaric kinglet, this cruel god, and the Jesus of Palm Sunday: same egoistic tyranny, same childish anger, same apparent justice (for a tree is judged by its fruits), but an imperturbable justice without pity that functions like a cleaver.

There we can measure Luke's daring: he puts his gardener Jesus opposite the little tyrannical god. A Jesus against a God!

For the gardener does not obey the Master. He does everything to save his tree. It is a parable of recovered freedom for the trees, even against God!

Yes, a formidable pamphlet, one that forces us to reconsider our rapport with God, our relation to God, and our religion.

I know well—and I am not proud of it—that I don't produce much fruit and that perhaps, in the eye of the Master, I don't deserve to occupy my place on earth. But it is the gardener, by his attitude and his intervention, who poses to God and to all of us a lucid and troubling question.

Why presume between you and God such a relation of consuming and exploitation? Is religion that? Is the meaning of your life to satisfy God's appetite and assuage his hunger? Is God truly the one whose joy is to devour you, strip you bare, take everything from you? I am quite aware that we only plant trees in order to take their fruit. But why should we have such a petty image of God?

Let's be clear. For whom and why is the fig tree created and planted in the garden? To assuage God's hunger or so that it can be a fig tree, living as it can its life as a fig tree? Here is my question. When he plants a man and a son of man does the Father plant it envisaging his future paternal exploitation or so that the son can step by step become, simply, a man and as he intends it?

This parable of Jesus asks us to never fear being at the mercy of an agriculturally exploiting God. God has no right of life and death over us. In no circumstance can God say to us: If you produce nothing, or not enough, I have nothing to do with you, you wastefully occupy my earth. Out! You will be cut down! It is a false god, this god of production, devourer of my hours, my days, my nights, my summers and my winters, my tears and my joys. A God who devours my fruits and my life.

Such would be the Parable of a Master-God who exploits his slaves, whose only purpose is to make God live! It is a parable of the kinglets of all times, proprietors of the soil, of the home ground where I grew up, of the sap which rises in me, of the air which I breathe, of all that is me and makes me live. Finally, with the right of life and death over all of that. Cut it down!

I love it that Luke makes Jesus pass over into the other camp, that of the gospel of freedom.

The gardener's reply: "I will dig about it and put down manure." This is a laughable intervention. To dig and spread manure will do nothing. Moreover, the fig tree is not on rocky or undeveloped land. It is planted in the garden of the Master where for sure the soil is regularly cultivated and groomed.

For my part, I believe that the gardener isn't concerned to get fruit from the fig tree so as to have a tree that suits the appetite of the Master. What is important for him at the moment is to gain time. "Give it another year," and then we will see. Yes, to gain time, and with delay after delay and reprieve after reprieve, get the right for a tree simply to be a tree, with or without fruit. Success is not to still and always please the Master with a tree that passes muster, but to do justice to the tree and to its right to occupy the earth.

I think that the gardener has no illusion about his remedy or about the Master. Next year, the Master will be there with his question: Now are there some figs? It is better, then, to go ahead with a remedy which isn't one. "If not, you can cut it down."

The gardener extracts a reprieve which gives him a grace period. And that is the power of this Parable. A gardener does everything—yes, everything—to help the trees triumph against their Master. He does not say, After a year you will have a docile tree with lots of figs. No! Rather, he says, In a year perhaps the son that you desired will have become a man. Who knows? Perhaps God will cease seeing humans as beings to exploit at will.

It takes great courage to propose to God such a change, in the name of Jesus and the Gospel.

Let it live for another year, not because of its works, but gratuitously, by pure grace!

Jesus: he takes the side of people. He comes to place himself between God and me, between God's demands and my right to occupy the earth.

Jesus: this distance between God and me, this grace period. I call on Jesus to intercede, to place himself between, to hollow out a space of grace for my life.

I sometimes ask myself, Whom do you serve? What are you doing with your life on this earth? Jesus has delivered me from all of these oppressing religious questions. He puts himself even unto death between me and these questions. He establishes my right to occupy the earth. He authorizes me. Yes, he authorizes me against all the gods, all the Masters.

He doesn't promise me heaven, but the earth, my corner of earth where I can live out my own history.

The Gospel of Luke: a parable never to forget.

Love Jesus and do as you please. You are free.
Friends, that is called grace!

19

A Story of Adultery

JOHN 8:3–11

The Scribes and the Pharisees brought a woman who had been caught in adultery, and making her stand before all of them, they said to him, "Teacher, this woman was caught in the very act of committing adultery. Now in the law Moses commanded us to stone such women. Now what do you say?" This they said to test him, so that they might have some charge to bring against him. Jesus bent down and wrote with his finger on the ground. When they kept on questioning him, he straightened up and said to them, "Let anyone among you who is without sin be the first to throw a stone at her." And once again he bent down and wrote on the ground. When they heard it, they went away one by one, beginning with the elders; and Jesus was left alone with the woman standing before him. Jesus straightened up and said to her, "Woman, where are they? Has no one condemned you?" She said, "No one, sir." And Jesus said, "Neither do I

> *condemn you. Go on your way, and from now on do not sin again."* NRSV

THIS FRAGMENT of the Gospel of John is a true jewel. Here we met an admirable Jesus.

They set a trap for him. The Pharisees, having brought a woman "caught in adultery," put a question to Jesus. "Moses commanded us to stone such. What do you say?" He could not reply that Moses is to be surpassed. If he did that, he would have been stoned on the spot!

We are in one of the interior courts of the Temple. The atmosphere is tense, tragic. Some are already carrying stones. Others, more sensitive, are upset, trembling with emotion. Someone is about to be put to death. The woman is frozen with fear. How can a gospel be announced here?

Jesus draws on the ground with his finger. This is a little like when he slept during a storm in the back of a boat in danger. Admirable Jesus. Peace. Nothing but peace. He is calm like pardon. He is strong like love. He is stronger than death and stronger than religion.

I am afraid of disturbing this strange calm by speaking. I would prefer to let Jesus continue to draw on the ground. May he pardon me for bothering him! I want to risk telling you three things that enchant me. First, I see that the author smiles. He, also, has drawn; on his page he has created a pamphlet against the super-masculine organization of this religious society. Next, I see Jesus smiling. He has found a way to parry; he will play Moses against Moses. Finally, and

A Story of Adultery

this no one will be able to forget, on the liberated woman is a smile irrigated by tears of gratitude.

Let's begin with the pamphlet, *the smile of the writer*. Around this woman pale with fear are nothing but men. Why must only men judge? Why is the woman the only one condemned? Adultery, caught in the act, necessarily involves both a woman and a man. And the pious men say in chorus: "Moses commanded us to stone such women." Not at all. Even Moses never said that. Here is what we can read in Deuteronomy 22:22: "Both of them shall die." Yes, both of them. And because the ancient law, which doesn't even have the word "mercy," covers all possible cases, it specifies: "If it happens in the open country, only the man will be punished by death." Only the man.

Pious men, full of self-importance and deceit. Vengeful males who gather in numbers to beat up on their female prey. There is nothing here but a blasphemous imitation of justice, masculine tyranny dressed up as religion.

Yes, the writer smiled. His story is well constructed. "Let anyone among you who is without sin be the first to throw a stone at her!" One by one the bullies must retreat before the Gospel. No one but men? Yes, when it is a matter of condemning. But one by one, they must retreat, pitifully retreat, in the presence of a woman! And Jesus takes his time, as shown by his drawing in the sand. And the men lose face by retreating before a woman. And also before Jesus, before the Pardon which is Jesus.

The entire super-masculine society is brought down: "Let anyone among you who is without sin be the first to throw a stone at her!" One blow, and the picture is erased. With two drops of love and pardon, all the masculine privileges crumble. "Woman" (this word so pejorative in Israel—but is it only in Israel?), said Jesus, "where are they?" "They," this glorious masculine plural, has it disappeared? "No one," answered the woman. One blows on the picture and it all goes away. It is a pamphlet that makes one smile while waiting for the Gospel.

And now, *the smile of Jesus.* Right under their noses he will so turn the Scriptures around that it will be hard to tell who are the torturers and where the adultery is to be found. When it comes to sins, one can talk only about one's own.

Where are the stones?, asks Jesus. Go ahead! Begin! What constitutes getting caught red-handed? Do you want to talk about Moses? There is a transgression here, but not the one you think. We have a case of idolatry. You speak of adultery, and you are right. For Scripture calls adultery the idolatry that serves a god other than the true God. And that is what you do when you serve a God that is strange to me, the God of punishment, of violence and of shed blood.

You have said adultery? Well, then, bring on the stones! Stoning, that is the ceremony of the idolaters! The real sin has been unmasked. Under the mask of religious judges there is nothing but torturers and adulterers! For they serve another god than the God of love. They have chosen a murderous God. This God of killers and sinners is a false god.

Jesus says, you are idolaters. With your taste for blood shed for the honor of God, you betray Moses and, even more, God himself. You have another God than Israel's. You are idolaters and, Moses says, adulterers.

This is a new reading of Moses. Idolaters are all those who invoke their God only better to denounce the sin of others and, if possible, to put them to death! They are murderous idolaters and servants of a God of death!

In every religious person who wishes to be sinless sleeps a murderer. Stoning is for whom? Is it for the woman and her accomplice because adultery is a deadly sin? Is it for the accusers who have changed God into an idol and turned their back to a merciful God to be replaced by a bloody God who would like to see the blood of sinners run? All are adulterers. This is clear for Moses as well as for Jesus: don't commit adultery; don't commit idolatry; and don't be mistaken about God. God is love, nothing but love.

And finally, *the tearful smile of the woman*. A future is still possible for her! "Go, and do not sin again!" She was dead, and there she is at the threshold of her resurrection.

Jesus rises. He speaks, and the entire gospel of freedom and forgiveness bursts forth like an Easter morning. This grand project of resurrection does not apply only to the woman (though above all for her), but also for others. If not, nothing has really happened. Grace must also be given to the torturers. It is always necessary to liberate both the victim and the torturer. This "Go!" is a personal singular, for every person.

Moreover, the text shows this, by a voluntary and organized inaccuracy. Once the crowd had left, when the religious idolaters had left the court, this is written: "The woman was still there, *in the middle*." In the middle of what? In the middle of whom?

Precisely, she is now an exemplary middle, exact center, and everyone is there, like her, in her, idolater or adulterer. Yes, she is alone, but she represents each one. She is what all are: nothing great, little person, idolater or adulterer. But she understands what is important for all: the promise. "Go, and do not sin again!"

It is as simple as Easter morning. Jesus launches us again. True justice does not concern yesterday (it neither accuses nor excuses), but promises a new tomorrow. Go! Move on! Sin no more! Kill no more! Go! I do not stone you. I resurrect you.

Someone had come to die. Someone had come to kill. But to them the Gospel is announced: it is called passion and empty tomb; it is called forgiveness.

Friend, I do not condemn you. I give you new life . . .

20

My Lord: It Is Like a Man Going on a Journey . . .

MARK 13:33–37

"Beware, keep alert; for you do not know when the time will come. It is like a man going on a journey, when he leaves home and puts his servants [for slaves] *in charge, each with his work, and commands the doorkeeper to be on the watch. Therefore, keep awake—for you do not know when the master of the house will come, in the evening, or at midnight, or at cockcrow, or at dawn or else he may find you asleep when he comes suddenly. And what I say to you I say to all: Keep awake!"* NRSV, amended.

THAT IS an upsetting gospel, a gospel that Jesus proposed very often and that, nonetheless, everyone almost immediately forgot: It is like a man who goes on a journey and gives all his power to his servants. That amounts to the gospel of the absent Lord!

On going through the Gospels, it is easy to see, this surprising situation is evoked numerous times. It is like a refrain, a constant that Jesus thereby underlines, and that we have nearly always neglected. It is a gospel that requires much courage to announce and much faith if one wants to live it.

The Lord that I am announcing to you is a Lord who goes away! Not because he doesn't think much of you; to the contrary, it is because he thereby wants to show how much he loves you. My God is like a man who goes on a journey and gives all his power to his servants.

Think of the parables. We often hear this same refrain.

The Parable of the Vineyard: a man planted a vineyard, then let it out to tenants and went into another country for a long while. . . . The Parable of the Talents: a man going on a journey called his servants and entrusted to them his property. . . . The Parable of the Pounds: a man of noble birth went into a distant country to be appointed king. . . . The Parable of the Master who sits his servants down at table to wait for him to return from the wedding feast. . . . It is true also of the Parables of the Foolish Virgins, the Doorkeeper, the Master of the Wedding, and also of the Shepherd who abandons his flock on the hillside to search in the desert. And it is true as well of the Sower who sowed good grain in his field, did nothing, allowed the Enemy to come and sow weeds, did not try to always be at the field, to always be "there"; thus a Sower who is not always there and chooses not to be.

My Lord: It Is Like a Man Going on a Journey... 111

Each time, Jesus proclaims the same gospel. In his parables, all these kings who go away, these shepherds who abandon, these masters and husbands who go afar, these noblemen off on a long trip, have one thing in common: they reveal the great secret of Jesus' God: "My God is a Lord who departs on a voyage and goes far away!" Not at all because he wants nothing more to do with you. To the contrary! It is because he loves you like no one in the world has ever loved you.

More than this, Jesus says: my God is the only one who is love, the only one who desires to confer everything to you when he goes on a trip, to hide himself in order to bestow all his authority on you. Thus, all initiative, all responsibilities, all risks, all choices, all rights are conferred on the servants.

In reality, each time, it turns out to be the Parable of the Autonomy of the Servants, based solely on the love of the Master. So, the Lord of this gospel says to his servants, it is up to you alone to respond for me and my project on my earth!

In other religions of the world, even the Jewish religion, even those who call themselves Christian, God, on the contrary, is always there, inevitable, unlimited, always occupying all the space. Nothing escapes him. No moment of the lives of his subjects is hidden from him. He controls all. He surveys all. He sees all. It is the great policeman who sees even hidden and secret things. He hears everything, even what is not said. The great unbearable inquisitor, omnipresent and all powerful. Jesus says, that is a false god (and such courage will lead to his death).

The agonizing presence of this all-powerful one confiscates absolutely all freedom and reduces his subjects to being only remote-controlled puppets, imbecilic automatons obeying all the orders coming from on high.

As for Jesus, he makes us love the God who is not there, because he has confidence in us and confers on us all authority over his house. The religious establishment of his time could not stand such a gospel for very long.

How is it that I accept it?

God says, I am going away. Live like free, responsible, and autonomous persons! Live like grownups! Dare to live without me! Throw yourselves into life like adults, and may each of you accomplish your task, your own work, your own identity, your personal life to invent and risk.

The Lord goes away. Like the father steps aside so that the son can advance. Like the mother backs away—but keeps her arms wide open—in front of the child staggering into its first steps. It is without her that the child will walk, and will be.

I will let go of your hand, says God. Live like grownups, because I love you.

Jesus here does no more than to celebrate the beautiful secret of the creation of humans sung in the old poem of the beginnings. My God, Jesus says, is like that creator on the seventh day: he will rest, apart. God's Day of Rest.

That is the masterpiece of the creation: not all the extraordinary marvels of the first six days (and yet, who could do better?), but his seventh day. Daring to leave, to withdraw and sleep, that's when God's masterpiece is achieved. That is the perfection of creation, this "doing nothing." For in withdrawing God creates the creature's freedom. In effect, this day of the absence of the creator will be the first day of free humanity. The poem of beginnings: God created humans the way the ocean created continents, by withdrawing.

Out of love, God hollows out in front of us a space of freedom so that we will not be overwhelmed by an exterior force (and thus disastrous, given the source).

The Master goes away and gives over all his authority. To me! He emancipates me. He decolonizes me. He makes me an adult, responsible, a full human! He authorizes me to be a free person. Is there a greater gospel?

To love is to make free the one you love. Only a great love, a love from God, could lead another to freedom. To love another not to possess them, master them, but to make them free; not to seduce them, but to expand them; not to cover them with emotional bonds that will smother them, but simply to wait in prayer at their door.

God of Jesus. God of my freedom. God weak and trembling like a lover. God foolish with love for me, renouncing all superiority, anxious but confident, feverish but faithful, waiting in prayer at my door. A Lord who goes on a journey.

In the Gospel of Mark, this is the very last parable of Jesus, his testament.

It was the end. He no longer had any illusions. Everyone challenged him, accused him, and plotted to put him to death. He knew not the day or the hour, but he kept vigil. He lived every word of his last parable. He also was about to depart for a long journey and leave his friends. That is why it was important for them to understand well his ultimate gospel; they were not going to be abandoned, but free and adult.

He would not be there, but also not far away: just on the other side of our freedom.

21

Christ is Born in Pagan Territory

MARK 7:24—9:10

From there he set out and went away to the region of Tyre. He entered a house and did not want to have anyone to know he was there. Yet he could not escape notice, but a woman whose little daughter had an unclean spirit immediately heard about him, and she came and bowed down at his feet. Now the woman was a Gentle, of Syrophoenician origin. She begged him to cast the demon out of her daughter. He said to her, "Let the children be fed first, for it is not fair to take the children's food and throw it to the dogs." But she answered him, "Sir, [Yes, Lord, RSV] even the dogs under the table eat the children's crumbs." Then he said to her, "For saying that, you may go—the demon has left your daughter." So she went home, found the child lying on the bed, and the demon gone. NRSV

Read also the account of Jesus' entire trip into pagan territory (7:31 to 9:10), which culminates

in Peter's confession of faith, "You are the Christ,"
and the celebrated Transfiguration narrative.

According to Mark, Jesus' ministry consisted of three major periods: at the beginning was the Galilean spring, a time of popular enthusiasm; at the end, a slow funeral march toward Jerusalem and the Cross; and in between a critical parenthesis when Jesus had an internal debate as if he wasn't sure which route to take. It is this critical period, emphasized only by Mark, that we will explore, although rapidly. The stakes are high. Is Jesus to be one of the prophets of Israel or a Christ openly turned toward the pagans, a "universal" Christ?

This exact center of the Gospel of Mark takes up two chapters and takes place *entirely beyond the frontier of Israel.* This grand voyage among the pagans, this kind of bath in profanity, marks the beginning of a new ministry, an other baptism, an other beginning. Jesus will get an other identity. This conversion will happen on pagan territory, not in Samaria or Decapolis but *in truly pagan countries.*

In what follows I will take up only the beginning of this new turn (his new birth), but it is worth noting all the decisive elements of the trip, because clearly it isn't just a matter of a trip but of a theological displacement of the Messiah outside the Holy Land. In Scripture only *Cyrus* was equally celebrated as the Messiah beyond the frontier. It was daring for Second Isaiah to call this Zoroastrian emperor of the Medes and the Persians "the man of God's Design," "Jahweh's shepherd," "the servant of God and his

Christ is Born in Pagan Territory 117

chosen son on whom his Spirit rests," in short, "the Christ," "the one the Lord loves."![1]

In this case, it is not a foreigner but it still is quite daring to salute Jesus as the Liberator of not just Jews, but also of all the pagans. We can all recognize here the great debate dividing the Church when the Gospel of Mark was written. Should Paul who preached to pagans be approved? Should one follow the church of the Seven at Antioch of Syria who evangelized Samaria and Decapolis rather than the church of the Twelve of Jerusalem and its judeo-christians?

It appears that Mark has taken the side of Paul and Antioch and that he wants to show, by Jesus' travels among the pagans, that, after all, they were only continuing what the Galilean had done.

Here, then, is a brief résumé of the *steps of the "conversion" of Jesus*. There are nine events, all occurring in pagan lands, that little by little produce for Jesus a *change of identity*.

1 – *In the region of Tyre*: an encounter with the pagan woman who will force Jesus to heal her daughter. This is the "birth" of Jesus because here he is "presented to the world." This is the decisive story that will be discussed later. (Mark 7:24–30.)

2 – *In the region of Sidon*: Jesus, face to face with a deaf-mute, recognizes himself in this disability. Hadn't he been deaf to the supplications of the imploring mother? Hadn't he lost his Word of hope and the Gospel? The episode ends

1. Isaiah 40:13; 44:28; 42:1; 45:1; 48:14.

with a beneficial realization. Two persons will be healed: the sick man and Jesus. And the crowd, witnessing a single healing, will exclaim: "He makes the deaf to hear and the mute to speak." In the plural! (Mark 7:31–37.)

3 – *Same region:* the multiplication of bread already done in Galilee for the inhabitants of Israel must be repeated, but this time for the pagans, only for the pagans. (Mark 8:1–10.)

4 – *Region of Dalmanutha*: no another sign, and Matthew and Luke specify that there will be no other sign than that of Jonah! That sign is not a humorous sign of a death followed by a resurrection out of the "stomach of a fish," but of the extravagant prophecy represented by the impossible mass entry into the people of God of the entire population of Nineveh, the worst pagans of the time. (Mark 8:11–13.)

5 – *Lakeside*: how should the Church understand the meaning of this second multiplication of bread? Jesus' question: at the multiplication for Israel, how many baskets of broken pieces did you collect? Response of the disciples: twelve. Second question: and how many at the multiplication in pagan country? Response: seven. So, you have gone from twelve to seven! Jesus underlines: from twelve to seven! "Do you not yet understand?' It is passing from the community of the Twelve of Jerusalem to that of the Seven of Antioch. Can it be any clearer? (Mark 8:14–21.)

6 – *At Bethsaida:* healing of blindness. Is it simply of one blind man, or perhaps of all the disciples, disabled and confused by their trip to foreign lands? (Mark 8:22–26.)

7 – *At Caesarea Philippi*, on the "road to Damascus": the test question. Who do people say that I am and *you,*

who do you say that I am? On pagan territory, Jesus hears: "You are the Christ!" Jesus can change his name, carry a new baptismal name: *Christ*. He accepts this new mission which openly turns him toward the pagans. Thus, topographically, but also theologically, Jesus is on a true "road to Damascus" some time before Paul. (Mark 8:27–33.)

8 – *On the road to Damascus*: to be called Christ is to go toward crucifixion. Equally, to follow Jesus, is to take up his cross. It is not a matter of choosing death, but of choosing, whatever it takes, openness to the pagans. Ever since the revolt, in year 6 of the Common Era, of the Judas called "the Christ of Galilee," Rome always intervenes at the slightest messianic movement. And Judas' messianic movement cost two thousand crucified. (Mark 8:34 to 9:1.)

9 – *The apotheosis in Trachonitis*. It is the Transfiguration on the "high mountain" of Hermon. Literally, it is the metamorphosis of Jesus. To undertake his "new" mission Jesus will take on a new face, a new shape. Literally, he will be transfigured and be joined with Moses and Elijah, the only two heroes beyond the frontier. Moses, the greatest figure in the Scriptures, never put foot on Holy Land; he is the hero from outside, the hero without boundaries. Elijah, the prophet par excellence, is also a man without a country. Born outside the Holy Land, he had to live his entire life outside the frontiers of Israel because he was condemned to death by Ahab and Jezebel. He is the expatriate hero.

Jesus is Transfigured. From now on, he is the Christ, alongside Moses and Elijah, neither of whom were of Israel. They were the voice of God speaking from pagan countries. (Mark 9:2–10.)

Thus, Jesus is born in Bethlehem, according to the prophets, or at Nazareth. But Christ is born with the pagans! Consequently, all is in place: the trip abroad is finished. Jesus adopts his new identity, that of being the liberator not only of the Jews but of the entire world.

Before concluding, let's go back to where we started: the decisive encounter with the Syrophoenician woman. That is where it all began.

A pagan mother in desperation throws herself at the feet of Jesus and asks him to heal her daughter. At Sarepta, in the same region, long ago a mother had also asked and obtained the healing of her son by imploring the prophet Elijah. Could Jesus be a new Elijah?

For the first time Jesus has just crossed the frontier, and everything began badly. Matthew notes: "He did not answer her at all." And when the woman insisted Jesus said brutally, "I was sent only to the lost sheep of the house of Israel." Wasn't Jesus just that, a Jewish prophet sent only to Jews? But, happily, here he is on the other side of the boundary. While there will he perhaps change his role?

The mother dares to insist, for she is fighting for her child. But Jesus abominably bounces between racism and scorn. Go away, you dogs and your sick puppies! The bread is for real people and not for the daughter of a dog!

Jesus is more Jewish than ever, a worse nationalist than a Pharisee and a worse racist than an Essene. Where, then, is the prophet of hope? I give my bread to those of my own house. Jesus says, I have nothing to toss to your kind of dog.

These are the first steps, difficult and sad, beyond the frontier. But the woman insists again: "Yes, Lord, even

Christ is Born in Pagan Territory 121

the dogs under the table eat the children's crumbs!" This humble prayer of the desperate mother works miracles. She heals Jesus and also her daughter. She "speaks" to Jesus. She evangelizes him, offers him his good news, his new way, his new identity, his new role. She has succeeded, in the full sense of the words, *"to bring Jesus into the world."*

Mary was the mother of Jesus. Here, this anonymous pagan woman is *the mother of Christ*. And it all resembles a Christmas story because it is by this pagan mother that the universal Christ, the Christ of the others, is born. As in the Christmas story we hear something like "let it be according to your will." Moreover, this pagan mother will be blessed among all women because she has brought into the world the Christ of the Jews *and* the pagans. The daughter is healed. The Son is born. The frontier has indeed been crossed. The crisis is over. Jesus was born in Bethlehem, or Nazareth, but the Christ of the others, *the Christ of the world*, has just been born in pagan territory.

This is a passage narrative, one of birth, of the suffering of childbirth.

We can guess that it took a long trip abroad, a true bath in profanity, a deep immersion in the pagan world for Jesus to put away his exclusive Jewishness in order to be transfigured and resurrected as a universal Liberator.

In any case, from this time forward, the New Covenant has begun. May everyone know it and rejoice in it. Christ is born with the pagans in order to open up for them the road to freedom!

22

The Temple Veil Torn from Top to Bottom

MARK 15:33–38

When it was noon, darkness came over the whole land until three in the afternoon. At three o'clock Jesus cried out with a loud voice, "Eloi, Eloi, lema sabachthani?" which means, "My God, my God, why have you forsaken me?" When some of the bystanders heard it, they said, "Listen, he is calling for Elijah." And someone ran, filled a sponge with sour wine, put it on a stick, and gave it to him to drink, saying, "Wait, let us see whether Elijah will come to take him down." Then Jesus gave a loud cry and breathed his last. And the curtain of the temple was torn in two, from top to bottom. NRSV

*A*T THE *same instant* on that Friday two decisive and ultimate events took place: in the Temple of Jerusalem the Temple veil tears from top to bottom, and on Golgotha a condemned man dies with the loud pathetic cry, "My God, my God, why have you forsaken me?'

At the same instant, two terrible tearings: in the city, at the heart of the city, the Temple veil; and outside the walls, on the periphery, the agonizing cry of the Son of Man. Two places, in the city and outside the city, the same putting to death destroys everything, from top to bottom, in the center and on the periphery.

I would like, as a thought experiment, to lead you from one of the places of this Friday to the other of this Friday that we call holy. I am about to take you on an imaginary pilgrimage from the center to the periphery on that Friday about three o'clock.

The Temple. Our point of departure: the center, the centrality, the holy place, *the beneficent sacred*, the positive pole of the City of David.

In reality, there are two veils here. The first (the one which tears from top to bottom) is the sacred veil par excellence, that which separates the holy place from the Holy of Holies. It is a veil not to be crossed. In fact, no one passes through it except, once a year, the chief sacrificer. This is where the pilgrimage begins.

What follows is a whole series of obstacles, for the route we take is a forbidden route. In fact, it is forbidden to join together the heart of the sacred Temple to the summit of Golgotha, *forbidden to join the beneficial sacred with the harmful sacred*. But it is the ninth hour. . . .

After this holy place, we must enter another protected space because it is a dangerous zone for lay people. We are going to come up against several barriers, part several curtains.

First there is the holy place of the priests, and whoever enters there who is not a priest must die! There is a door closed at night and a veil (a second veil) drawn day and night.

Beyond a vestibule reserved for only priests we come to a first court open to the sky and thus, in reality, to a series of interior courts, each one enclosed within a larger court which protects it. From court to court, from curtain to curtain, we are gradually desacralized. First the court of the priests, then the court of men, then the court of women. We have come nearly to the external boundary of the sacred! For after the court of women there is the general enclosure of the Temple, a vast and very particular space, like an enclave of Holy Ground that even the lowliest occupants always respect as the ultimate place of the autonomy of Israel.

Thus we are there in the last sanctified space, because on the other side of the wall is the profane, the city. And on the walls are placed signs, in Greek and Latin, forbidding entry to the Temple of any stranger, any non-Jew, under pain of death.

The city, certainly, is not a truly holy place, but neither is it totally profane, for it is Jerusalem, the City of David. But after this final step down, on leaving the city we enter the "world."

We have now gone half the way, the clear half. From now on we begin the slow progression toward the damned. With the same precautions as before, little by little, we must walk toward the other sacred, as untouchable as the first, *the evil sacred.*

This begins from the time we are "outside the walls." We had to cross a fearsome barrier. There is nothing in common between the inside and the outside, because the outside is the darkness, this sorrowful and dramatic zone of the lepers who do not have the right to enter the city, who are neither dead nor alive, neither totally damned nor completely savable. This is the first degree of the darkness.

Next comes the region of the tombs where the graves are bright white so that they can be avoided. Then, and even if we are climbing, is the descent into Hell. It is Golgotha, the land of ritual murder, with the symbol of cursedness: a gallows in the form of the cross. It is worse than Gehenna where cadavers and refuse continually burn, for here there is groaning and suffering.

On a cross the cry of the condemned tears through a strange night that arrives in full daylight. We have reached the final stop of our pilgrimage when we arrive at this evil sacred place in all its horror, the holy anti-place, at the antipodes from the first veil, separated from it by all those impassable obstacles. But the Gospel says that on this Friday, there and here, the there so far away, in this there so opposed and so contrary to this here, *there and here, at the same time, the same tearing from top to bottom!*

At the foot of the Cross, with the three synoptic gospels, we must celebrate the end of the entire sacred organization of Israel. Everything is torn. Everything is brought down to the ground. It is the end of this topography of the lawful and unlawful sacred. Everything is at the same level. No more sacred at all.

In the two places—the supersaturated holy place of the *presence* of God as well as the cursed place where the *absence* of God is taken to its extreme—we have the end, the death, the tearing from top to bottom of the side of the king as well as the side of the leper. For that is the Gospel. The only king is leprous, for the leper is king. And God is the dead and abandoned Son .

The secret of God is "unveiled." God has no more secrets. God is fully visible, face to face, not behind a veil but without a veil, *naked on a cross.*

God without secrets. God's holy place was empty, like an empty tomb. God is public, a crucified in front of a crowd.

The torn veil, that is, the end of religious organizations, the sacred art of excluding and separating. There is no longer the lawful sacred necessary to triumph over the unlawful sacred. The Gospel is the story of the possibility of people reconciled and reunited, delivered from all the sacreds, the good and the bad.

The torn veil more dramatically is the mask of God that falls. And behind? Nothing other than an innocent man who is tortured and who dies, all alone, in front of a crowd.

Now is the time to be absolutely clear about the meaning of the cross. Jesus has not "penetrated the veil" (as the epistle to the Hebrews will say). He is not a sovereign sacrifice. He did not offer a sacrifice. To the contrary, his death has torn the veil from top to bottom, has made it a derisory and irreparable piece of fabric.

Jesus has not offered the perfect sacrifice of expiation. No! Sacrifice is still in the economy of the sacred, and it is precisely this religious universe that was abolished, torn through his death.

Our hymns and liturgies that speak continually of the "blood that purifies" are wrong because they keep us religious prisoners of the categories of the sacred. Reread the gospels carefully: there is not a single drop of blood! Blood isn't introduced until the end of the first century with the epistle to the Hebrews and the fourth gospel with its "blow of the sword." The torn veil also tells us that there is no blood that purifies and no sacrifice on the cross. This is true, at least according to the original account of the first three evangelists . . .

Who can escape? All of this accuses us.

All of us who are religious from head to foot, who unceasingly sew up the torn veil, we divide the world into multiple sacreds, we reinvent the geographies of salvation and the subtle religions of sacrifice.

Worse! With that we rob Jesus of his own death. Dead for nothing?

His death has torn the veil of the Temple, and we, by celebrating his death as a sacrifice that saves us, as a lawful sacred act that heals us from the unlawful, we already sew up over his still warm cadaver the veil that he tore only by his death. The veil is torn. Did Jesus die for nothing?

Brothers and sisters, beware not to still steal his death from him!

It was the ninth hour, there and here.

God no longer has secrets. God's mask has fallen. There is no longer any sacred, no lawful and unlawful. Never again will there be temple or sacrifice. God is called Son of Man among us. He sends us a sign of this every time a wall is torn down and each time that one of the little ones of his friends groans near to us.

23

Easter: His Body has Disappeared!

MARK 16:1–8[1]

When the Sabbath was over, Mary Magdalene, and Mary the mother of James, and Salome bought spices, so that they might go and anoint him. And very early on the first day of the week, when the sun had risen, they went to the tomb. They had been saying to one another, "Who will roll away the stone for us from the entrance to the tomb?" When they looked up, they saw that the stone, which was very large, had already been rolled back. As they entered the tomb, they saw a young man, dressed in a white robe, sitting on the right side; and they were alarmed. But he said to them, "Do not be alarmed; you are looking for Jesus of Nazareth, who was crucified. He has been raised; he is not here. Look, there is the place they laid him. But go, tell his disciples and Peter that he is going ahead of you to Galilee; there you will see him, just as he told you." So they went out and fled from the tomb, for terror and amazement had

1. According to the best manuscripts, the Gospel of Mark ends here: "They said nothing to anyone, for they were afraid." *Period*!

> *seized them; and they said nothing to anyone, for they were afraid.* NRSV

It is Mark's sobriety that moves me and really evangelizes me. I am close to thinking that notions such as the finale added to the Our Father ("the kingdom and the power and the glory") or those of majesty, throne, and judgment have not been sufficiently "evangelized" and carry too much vainglory and self-importance to correctly reflect what we know of the life of the Nazarene who came not to be served, but to serve. But his Resurrection and exaltation constitute a formidable trap for us. Is it possible to resist the temptation to reintroduce, now that he is no longer here to respond, the images of praise and adulation that Jesus rejected during his teaching? To put it another way, is this really "my" Jesus who restores life, humble servant, weighed down with flesh and blood, with weariness and worries, passionate for the little ones and the poor? Yes, is this really *the one who will restore life, or rather, someone completely different*, surprising, rich, magisterial, huge and unexpected, yes, completely different? So here is my question: Will the Gospel of the man of Nazareth be confirmed or annulled by the arrival of a too powerful Lord of glory?

In any case, on this point, the Gospel of Mark is perfectly exemplary. Very little of the marvelous. No self-sufficiency, no outburst of heavenly fever. We are given only the simple observation: *his body has disappeared*. Period. "You are looking for Jesus of Nazareth, who was crucified.

He has been raised; he is not here. Look, there is the place they laid him."

Here is the essence of the Gospel: the disappearance of the body of Jesus on Easter morning. General frustration. Since Friday evening, no one had the body. No seizing of it. Unfindable. Untouchable. No one in the world, ever!

With a body, even unrecognizeable, one could adapt. We could "recover" it, take it with us to our gatherings, make it walk with us the roads to Emmaus or on the beach on a morning when the fishing is bad. In short, "still have him a little bit"! We wouldn't be left with empty hands!

Like Mary Magdalene and the other women, we could perhaps have embalmed him with spices and noble hymns, placed him carefully in a brand new tomb or in very old liturgies and memorable rituals. Or even, who knows, put him in welcoming shelters where a meal is shared or solidly nailed him to a wooden cross. That way it would have been possible to "keep him a little bit" and render homage to him. One could seriously think religiously, with ardor, as is proper for an entire holy week or two or three or even forty days! But, wait: his body has disappeared! With the Gospel of Mark, it is impossible to keep him "for a little while." Nothing. Nothing but the declaration: he has disappeared!

"Look, there is the place they laid him." Is it possible to launch a quest for this disappeared body?

I know that Jesus' goal was not to disappear that way and leave us with empty hands. To the contrary, he wished to live fully by giving himself, and give all by living. His goal was to invent a new life: to be only what one gives. By him, human life became possible.

But from the beginning no one was in support of this new way of living. People responded to his declaration in the synagogue of Nazareth[2] by trying to kill him by throwing him off a cliff.

His body? It is with his body that he began to disappear, that he began to let himself be dispossessed. His life was a long death of three years. It was a slow disappearing, a slow using up. He was love. He spoke it, he lived it, he was it. For love is always a dying, a dying to self, an abandon of self.

One day, he found himself almost totally given, stripped, empty from having given all through love. So, when death came, there was almost nothing for it to take, to carry off, not even a body. At the end, he had reached the peak of his love, and no one could find his body.

It is all along that dying of three years that the quest for the disappeared body must take place. That is the place to search and "to see where he has been laid." There first of all.

Three years to "have not yet died" so as to continue preaching the Kingdom. Three years to still "survive" and always to give and to love. Three years to rise up anew each morning, and each morning resurrected; each morning is already Easter day!

It was well before the end that Jesus won life over death. Well before the end that he had already walked on water and calmed its force; that he had battled the storm and the winds; that he had raised the dead and the poor; that he had liberated the lepers and the rich; that he had celebrated the festival of broken bread beyond the limit of possibility. He had already every day shown that to forgive was after

2. Luke 4:16ff.

all only to give above all, to radically give all, to give back absolutely everything. From the beginning of his ministry, Easter was there, and his new life. Everywhere already was the life which won. "Come see" all these places where his life was placed and displaced in order to reanimate towns and countrysides of Galilee and Judea. The search for the disappeared body is not over. He has also been "placed" in Galilee, and there, you will see for sure that since a long time he has "preceded you there." There are still many disabled and sick there for whom Jesus has obtained the triumph of life over death!

Thus this search for the disappeared body tells us the story of the present reality of the Resurrected One among us. That is why the quest for the Resurrected One must not deal only with the story of the Nazarene, but also with ours, our present time. In fact, I believe that the Resurrected One inhabits incognito our world, speaks there, works there, and prays there.

Yes, I know that the Resurrected One lives among us, not as a glorious and magnificent king, but as a servant, a friend of the poor and the excluded, the little ones and the forgotten. As before, yes, the same Jesus as before!

Where is the Resurrected One today; where precisely are these liberating actions? No one can say for sure. But no one can nor no one must (at least if they claim to belong to Jesus) refuse to try to give a concrete answer to these difficult questions.

To live Easter today is to put oneself on the quest for the Resurrected One in our cities and in our lives.

Let each of us search for the signs of his presence and of his intervention acting among us!

The quest is delicate, hit and miss, confusing, risky. Should it be prepared for with several others? But it is up to each to dare their own interpretation. Each one is to commit, in fear and trembling, to go rejoin him, he who always goes ahead of us and always already works to make life triumph over death.

To believe in Easter is perhaps only that: for each one to discover where the Living One awaits. Then, to go there, among others, familiar and different, to offer a little of his or her time, bread, muscle (the heart is also a muscle), and hope. The Beautiful Gospel of Mark: he has disappeared; go then all of you to search for him!

That is called the dawn. For Easter is always a morning.

www.ingramcontent.com/pod-product-compliance
Lightning Source LLC
Chambersburg PA
CBHW072147160426
43197CB00012B/2278